# DICTIONARY OF SYNONYMS, ANTONYMS, HOMONYMS & HETERONYMS

# DICTIONARY OF SYNONYMS, ANTONYMS, HOMONYMS & HETERONYMS

**Prof. Shakti Batra**
Deptt. of English
Dyal Singh College
(University of Delhi)
New Delhi-110 003

**ANMOL PUBLICATIONS PVT LTD**
**New Delhi-110 002**

**ANMOL PUBLICATIONS PVT LTD**
4374/4B, Ansari Road, Daryaganj
New Delhi-110 002

*Dictionary of Synonyms, Antonyms, Homonoyms & Heteronyms*

Reprint 1993
Reprint 1994
Reprint 1995
**Reprint 1996**

**PRINTED IN INDIA**

Published by J.L. Kumar for Anmol Publications Pvt Ltd, New Delhi-110 002 and Printed at Mehra Offset Press, Delhi.

# INTRODUCTION

This addition to the cluster of dictionaries in various disciplines is intended as an aid to vocabulary building. It incorporates not only widely used synonyms and antonyms, but also includes separate sections on Homonys and Heteronyms (generally covered under the larger heading: Words Often Confused and Misused of Pairs of Words). Alphabetically arranged entries provide an easy reference to head words in order to enable you to express an idea in different words so that repetition ( and the resultant monotony ) is avoided. It also enables to use the right word in the right context and at the right time. The verbal wealth in the world's most prevalent language has been carefully culled and selected to enable you to possess the faculty of fluent sum of expression.

Synonyms and antonyms play a significant part in improving one's expression. The first section seeks to provide you with a wide choice of such expressions in their subtle shades. The appendage giving homonyms and heteronyms is something that has not been attempted by any Indian publication so far. This is, thus, a dictionary as well as a thesarus. Much larger dictionaries on the subject may be available, but they often end up by confusing the user by giving providing long and unwidely lists of complicated, often rare, words as well as other technicalities. The best use of this dictionary is to remind the user of words he cannot think of when they are needed. It is intended as a guide to commonly used words in English, and those are almost always the most expressive. Used with good judgment, this book should yield both results.

# SYNONYMS & ANTONYMS

## A

***Abandon*** : *vb.* 1. leave, quit; desert, forsake; 2. give up, surrender; *adv. phr.* ***with abandon*** freely, unrestrainedly, without restraint, control, inhibition, or constraint; *Ant.* join, engage, unite, embrace, retain.

***Abandoned*** : *adj.* wicked, depraved, evil; immoral; *Ant.* righteous, virtuous.

***Abbreviate*** : *vb.* shorten, abridge, cut, reduce, condense; *Ant.* lengthen, extend, augment.

***Abie*** : *adj.* 1. capable, qualified, fit, competent; 2. *talented,* skilled, clever, skillful; *Ant.* unable, incompetent

***Abnormal*** : *adj.* unusual, uncommon, odd, peculiar, queer; strange, weird; *Ant.* normal, average, usual.

***Abode*** : *n.* See *dwelling*

***Abolish*** : *vb.* end, obliterate, erase, put out, eliminate; *Ant.* establish.

***Abominable*** : *adj.* hateful, loathsome, bad, terrible, awful, nasty, unpleasant; *Ant.* admirable, fine, noble.

***About*** : *prep.* 1. concerning, relating, involving.

***Above*** : *prep.* over, higher than, superior to; *Ant.* below, under, beneath.

***Abridge*** : *vb.* shorten, cut, abbreviate, abstract; *Ant.* expand, extend, increase.

***Abrupt*** : *adj.* 1. sudden, short; 2. short, curt, blunt, brusque, hasty, rude; 3. steep, sudden; *Ant.* gradual.

***Absence*** : *n.* want, need, lack; *Ant.* presence, existence.

***Absent*** : *adj.* 1. away, not present, out off; 2. missing, lacking, non-existent; *Ant.* present.

***Absent-minded*** : *adj.* forgetful; inattentive, wool-gathering, day-dreaming; *Ant.* alert, attentive.

***Absolute*** : *adj.* 1. perfect, whole, complete, unqualified, total; 2. total, complete, unlimited, limitless, unrestricted, arbitrary, tyrannical, dictatorial; *Ant.* partial, limited, fragmentary, incomplete.

***Absolutely*** : *adv.* definitely, positively, really, doubtelessly; *Ant.* uncertainly, doubtfully.

***Absolve*** : *vb.* acquit, exonerate, free from blame or responsibility (for), excuse, forgive, pardon, clear; *Ant.* accuse, charge.

***Absorb*** : *v.* 1. consume, occupy; 2. suck up, sop up, take in or up; *Ant.* 2. leak, drain.

***Absurd*** : *adj.* foolish, ridiculous, preposterous, laughable, silly; *Ant.* sensible, sound, reasonable.

***Abundance*** : *n.* plenty, copiousness, ampleness, profusion; *Ant.* scarcity, want, dearth, absence.

***Abundant*** : *adj.* plentiful, abounding, copious, profuse; *Ant.* scarce, rare, uncommon, absent.

***Accept*** : *vb.* 1. receive, take; 2. admit, allow, consent to; *Ant.* refuse, reject, ignore.

***Accommodate*** : *vb.* 1. aid, assist, help; 2. provide for, house, serve, hold; *Ant.* 1. inconvenience.

***Accompany*** : *vb.* escort, go with, join, attend; *Ant.* abandon, leave, forsake.

***Accomplish*** : *vb.* do, complete, achieve, fulfil, perform, finish, realise; *Ant.* fail.

***Accord*** : *vb.* 1. agree, concur; 2. award, grant, reward with, give; *n.* agreement, concord; *Ant. n.* disagreement, difference, quarrel.

***Accurate*** : *adj.* precise, correct, exact, right, true; *Ant.* inaccurate, inexact, mistaken, wrong.

***Accuse*** : *vb.* blame, charge, incriminate; *Ant.* absolve, clear.

***Accustomed*** : *adj.* (usually fol. by to) used to, familiar with, comfortable with; in the habit of; *Ant.* unfamiliar, strange.

***Achieve*** : *vb.* 1. do, perform, complete, accomplish, reach, realise 2. attain, gain, acquire, secure, procure; *Ant.* fail.

***Acid*** : *adj.* 1. sour, tart, vinegar-like; 2. sardonic, sarcastic, bitter, biting; *Ant.* 1. sweet, bland, mild.

***Acknowledge*** : *vb.* 1. agree to, admit, allow, concede, accept, grant; 2. accept, receive, express thanks *or* gratitude for, thank for, *Ant.* deny, refuse, reject.

***Acquaintance*** : *n.* associate, colleague, companion; *Ant.* stranger.

***Acquire*** : *vb.* obtain, procure, secure, get, gain, appropriate; *Ant.* lose, forfeit.

***Acquit*** : *vb.* excuse, forgive, exonerate, find not guilty, *Ant.* condemn, sentence.

***Active*** : *adj.* 1. energetic, vigorous, industrious; 2. busy, occupied, engaged; *Ant.* 1. lazy, lethargic, inactive.

***Actual*** : *adj.* real, true, genuine, certain; *Ant.* unreal, pretended, fake, bogus, false.

***Acute*** : *adj.* 1. severe, piercing, sudden; 2. sharp, keen, quick, perceptive, discerning, intelligent; *Ant.* 1. mild, bland. 2. insensitive, obtuse.

***Add*** : *vb..* 1. increase, supplement, augment; 2. total; *Ant.* subtract, remove, withdraw.

***Adequate*** : *adj.* sufficient, enough; satisfactory, fit, suitable; *Ant.* inadequate, insufficient.

***Adhere*** : *vb.* 1. cling, stick, hold; cleave; 2. be attached, be faithful, be devoted; *Ant.* 1. separate, loosen.

***Adherent*** : *n.* supporter, follower; *Ant.* defector, renegade, dropout.

***Adjacent*** : *adj.* near, next (to), close (to), neighbouring, nearby; *Ant.* apart, separate, distant.

***Adjoining*** : *adj.* close to, near, near to, next, next to, touching, bordering; *Ant.* separate, distant, remote.

***Adjourn*** : *vb.* suspend, postpone, put off; defer, delay; *Ant.* assemble, convene, begin.

***Admirable*** : *adj.* excellent, fine, worthy, praiseworthy; *Ant.* contemptible, despicable, sorry.

***Admiration*** : *n.* wonder, awe, pleasure, approval, esteem; *Ant.* contempt, disdain, disrespect.

***Admire*** : *vb.* revere, esteem, venerate, like, find praiseworthy or desirable; *Ant.* dislike, loathe, detest, hate.

***Admit*** : *vb.* 1. confess, acknowledge, own; 2. let in, allow to enter; *Ant.* 1. deny. 2. obstruct, reject.

***Admonish*** : *vb.* 1. warn, caution, advise against: 2. reprimand, rebuke, censure, reprove; *Ant.* praise, glorify.

***Ado*** : *n.* fuss, trouble, bother, to-do, bustle, flurry, activity, commotion, stir, excitement, upset, hubbub, confusion, tumult, turmoil; *Ant.* quietude, tranquillity.

***Adolescent*** : *adj.* teen-aged, teen-age, young, youthful, immature; *n.* teen-ager, youth, young person; *Ant. adj.* adult, grown, mature.

***Adore*** : *vb.* love, idolise, worship, revere, venerate, respect, honour, esteem; *Ant.* despise, hate, loathe.

***Adorn*** : *vb.* decorate, ornament, beautify, enhance, embellish; *Ant.* strip, bare.

***Adroit*** : *adj.* skillful, clever, adept, dexterous, ingenious, expert; *Ant.* clumsy, awkward, oafish, graceless.

***Adult*** : *adj.* mature, of age, full-grown; *n.* man, woman, grown-up;. *Ant. adj.* immature, infantile.

***Advance*** : *vb.* 1. proceed, progress, move, bring, *or* go forward; 2. further, promote; *n.* 1. progress, forward movement, advancement, improvement, promotion; 2. promotion, improvement, upgrade, upgrading, rise; *Ant. vb.* 1. retreat, withdraw, flee. 2. retard, obstruct. *n.* 1. retreat, retardation, withdrawal.

***Advantage*** : *n.* 1. favour, vantage, edge; 2. profit, gain, benefit; *Ant.* disadvantage, hindrance, loss.

***Adversary*** : *n.* opponent, antagonist, foe, enemy, contestant; *Ant.* friend, ally.

***Adverse*** : *adj.* 1. unlucky, unfortunate unfavourable; 2. contrary, opposite, opposing, opposed; *Ant.* 1. beneficial, favourable.

***Adversity*** : *n.* trouble, misfortune, distress, calamity, disaster, catastrophe; *Ant.* happiness, benefit.

***Advisable*** : *adj.* prudent, sensible, wise, proper, suitable, fit, fitting *Ant.* inadvisable, illconsidered, imprudent.

***Advocate*** : *vb.* support, recommend, argue *or* plead in favour of; *n.* supporter, promoter, upholder; *Ant. vb.* opponent, foe, adversary.

***Affect*** : *vb.* 1. modify, alter, change, transform; *A change in the speed limit affected everyone's drawing habits. 2. impress stir, move touch: The death of Jennie's kitten affected her deeply.*

***Affection*** : *n.* liking, fondness, attachment, friendliness, warmth, tenderness; *Ant.* dislike, aversion, antipathy.

***Affectionate*** : *adj.* fond, tender, attached, warm, loving; *Ant.* cold, distant, unfeeling.

***Affirm*** : *vb.* 1. declare, state, assert, say; 2. confirm, establish; *Ant.* 1. deny, disclaim.

***Affliction*** : *n.* 1. trouble, distress, grief, misfortune; 2. pain, suffering, misery, sickness, ailment, *Ant.* 1. benefit. 2. relief, easement.

***Afraid*** : *adj.* frightened, fearful, scared, terrified; *Ant.* confident, courageous, bold.

***Aged*** : *adj.* old, elderly, ancient; *Ant.* young, youthful.

***Aggravate*** : *vb.* intensify, worsen, make worse or more severe, heighten; *Ant.* ease, relieve, soothe.

***Aggressive*** : *adj.* 1. attacking, pugnacious, ready to fight, offensive; 2. active, vigorous, energetic, enterprising, determined; *Ant.* passive, shy, timid, withdrawn.

***Agile*** : *adj.* active nimble, graceful, lively, light on one's feet, spry; *Ant.* clumsy, awkward, inept.

***Agitate*** : *vb.* 1. shake, jar, shake up, toss, disturb; 2. stir up, excite, disturb; *Ant.* calm, soothe.

***Agree*** : *vb.* 1. settle, concur, harmonise, unite; 2. assent, consent, yield, concede; *Ant.* 1. disagree, argue. 2. refuse.

***Agreeable*** : *adj.* friendly, cooperative, pleasing, pleasant; *Ant.* disagreeable, quarrelsome, contentious, touchy.

***Agreement*** : *n.* 1. treaty, pact: deal, bargain, contract, understanding, arrangement; 2. settlement, accord, concord; *Ant.* disagreement, discord, misunderstanding.

***Aid*** : *vb.* help, assist, support, back; *n.* help, assistance, support, backing; *Ant. vb.* impede, obstruct, hinder, *n.* obstacle, hindrance.

***ailing*** *adj.* sick, ill, sickly; *Ant.* well, hearty, hale.

***Air*** : *n.* 1. atmosphere; 2. manner, appearance, character, look, attitude; *vb.* 1. ventilate; 2. display, publicise, expose, reveal; *Ant. vb.* 2. hide, conceal.

***Alarm*** : *n.* 1. fright, fear, dismay; 2. siren, bell, gong; *vb.* frighten, scare, terrify, startle; *Ant. vb.* calm. soothe comfort.

***Alarming*** : *adj.* shocking, appalling, daunting *Ant.* soothing, comforting, calming.

***Alert*** : *adj.* 1. watchful, attentive, vigilant, keen, wide-awake, observant; 2. quick, lively, active, spirited, bright; *n.* alarm, warning; *Ant. adj.* listless, dulled, sluggish, logy.

***Alien*** : *n.* foreigner, immigrant; stranger; *adj.* foreign, strange; non-native; *Ant. adj.* familiar, commonplace, accustomed.

***Allay*** : *vb.* quiet, soothe, calm, lessen, lighten, soften, moderate; *Ant.* arouse, worsen, intensify.

***Allege*** : *vb.* declare, affirm, state, assert: *Ant.* deny.

***Allegiance*** : *n.* loyalty, faithfulness, duty, obligation; *Ant.* disloyalty, treachery.

***Allow*** : *vb.* 1. permit let; 2. grant, cede, concede; 3. set aside or apart, provide for; *Ant.* 1. forbid, prohibit.

***Ally*** : *n.* associate, friend, partner; *vb.* 1. associate, join, unite; 2. unite, unify, combine, connect, join; *Ant. n.* enemy, foe, adversary.

***Almost*** : *adv.* nearly, somewhat; *Ant.* absolutely, completely.

***Alone*** : *adj.* lone, apart, separate, isolated; *adv.* solely, solo, solitarily; exclusively; *Ant. adv.* accompanied, together.

***Aloof*** : *adj.* distant, uninvolved, uninterested, withdrawn, separate, disdainful; *Ant.* friendly, outgoing, cordial, warm.

***Alter*** : *vb.* change, modify, vary; adjust; *Ant.* keep, preserve.

***Alteration*** : *n.* change, modification, difference, adjustment; *Ant.* preservation, maintenance.

***Alternate*** : *vb.* interchange, rotate; *Ant.* fix.

***Altitude*** : *n.* height, elevation; *Ant.* depth.

***Always*** : *adv.* forever, everlastingly, eternally, ever, forevermore; *Ant.* never, rarely.

***Amateur*** : *n.*novice, non-professional, tyro, beginner; *Ant.* professional.

***Amaze*** : *vb.*astonish, astound, surprise, stun, dumbfound; *Ant.* bore, tire, disinterest.

***Ambiguous*** : *adj.* unclear, uncertain, vague, deceptive; *Ant.* clear, unmistakable, certain.

***Amiable*** : *adj.* friendly, amicable, good-natured, outgoing, agreeable, kind-hearted, kind, pleasant; *Ant.* disagreeable, ill-tempered, cross, captious, touchy.

***Amiss*** : *adv.* improperly, wrongly, astray, awry; adj. improperly, wrongly, astray, awry; *adj.* improper, wrong, faulty; *Ant. adv.* properly, correctly, rightly; *adj.*right, correct.

***Ample*** : *adj.* 1. spacious, large, great, roomy; 2. liberal, abundant, plentiful; *Ant.* 1. cramped, confined. 2. insufficient, inadequate.

***Amplify*** : *vb.* enlarge, extend, broaden, develop, expand; *Ant.* restrict, confine, narrow, abridge.

***Amuse*** : *vb.*entertain, please, charm, divert; *Ant.* bore, tire.

***Amusement*** : *n.*entertainment, pastime, diversion, enjoyment, recreation, pleasure; *Ant.* boredom, tedium.

***Amusing*** : *adj.*entertaining, pleasing, pleasant, funny, comical; *Ant.* boring, tiring, tedious.

***Ancestry*** : *n.* lineage, descent, line, family, house; *Ant.* posterity.

***Anchor*** : *vb.*fasten, fix, pin; *Ant.* loosen, free, detach.

***Ancient*** : *adj.*antique, old, aged, old-fashioned, primitive; *Ant.* new, fresh, recent, current.

***Angel*** : *n.* seraph, cherub, archangel; *Ant.* devil, demon.

***Angry*** : *adj.* furious, mad, inflamed, irate, wrathful; *Ant..*

happy, content, tranquil.

***Anguish*** : *n.* pain, suffering, misery, distress, torment, agony; *Ant.* joy, ecstasy, pleasure.

***Animate*** : *vb.* enliven, vitalise, invigorate, stimulate; *adj.* alive, lively, vital, vigorous; *Ant. adj.* inanimate, dead.

***Announce*** : *vb.* proclaim, declare, report, publish, publicise; *Ant.* suppress.

***Annoy*** : *vb.* bother, irritate, irk, pester, harry, harass, disturb; *Ant.* comfort, soothe, please.

***Antagonism*** : *n.* hostility, enmity, opposition, conflict, animosity; *Ant.* friendliness, geniality, cordiality.

***Antagonist*** : *n.* adversary, opponent, rival, enemy, foe; *Ant.* friend, ally.

***Antique*** : *n.* objet diart, rarity, curio; *adj.* old, ancient, early, antiquated, old-fashioned, out-of-date, pass; *Ant. adj.* new, fresh, recent.

***Anxiety*** : *n.* uneasiness, distress, worry, foreboding, apprehension; *Ant.* peacefulness, placidity, calmness, tranquillity.

***Anxious*** : *adj.* worried, troubled, concerned, uneasy, apprehensive, fearful; *Ant.* peaceful, tranquil, calm.

***Apologetic*** : *adj.* regretful, sorry; *Ant.* unrepentant.

***Appall*** : *vb.* horrify, shock, dismay, frighten; *Ant.* please, edify.

***Apparent*** : *adj.* 1. plain, evident, clear, obvious, transparent, understandable; 2. seeming; *Ant.* 2. real, actual, evident.

***Appeal*** : *n.* 1. request, plea, petition, entreaty; 2. attraction, draw; *vb.* 1. request, plead, petition, entreat, beseech; 2. attract; *Ant. vb.* 2. repel, repulse.

***Appear*** : *vb.* 1. seem, look, 2. emerge, arise, turn up, arrive *Ant.* 2. disappear, vanish, evaporate.

***Appearance*** : *n.* 1. look, mien, aspect; 2. arrival presence;

*Ant.* 2. disappearance, vanishing.

***Applaud*** : *vb.* praise, approve (of), acclaim; *Ant.* disapprove, criticise, condemn, denounce.

***Applicable*** : *adj.* usable, fitting, suitable, proper, fit, appropriate, suited, *Ant.* inapplicable, inappropriate.

***Apply*** : *vb.* use, utilise, employ, make use of, put to use; *Ant.* neglect, ignore.

***Appoint*** : *vb.* 1. assign, nominate, name, designate, elect, establish, place; 2. determine, settle fix; *Ant.* 1. dismiss, discharge, fire.

***Appointment*** : *n.* 1. engagement, meeting, rendezvous; 2. assignment, designation, position; *Ant.* 2. dismissal, discharge.

***Appreciate*** : *vb.* 1. prize, value, be grateful for; 2. recognise, understand; *Ant.* 1. scorn, depreciate, undervalue.

***Apprehend*** : *vb.* 1. arrest, catch, seize, capture; 2. understand, perceive, grasp; *Ant.* 1. lose.

***Apprehension*** : *n.* 1. uneasiness, worry, fear, fearfulness, misgiving, dread, anxiety, anticipation; 2. arrest, capture, seizure; *Ant.* 1. composure, self-assuredness, confidence.

***Apprentice*** : *n.* learner, beginner, amateur, recruit *Ant.* master, professional.

***Appropriate*** : *adj.* fitting, proper, suitable; *vb.* assign, apportion, authorise; *Ant. adj.* inappropriate, unfit, inapt.

***Approve*** : *vb.* 1. praise, commend, appreciate; 2. authorise, sanction, endorse, confirm; *Ant.* 2. disapprove, deny.

***Apt*** : *adj.* 1. proper, suitable, fitting, appropriate, fit, suited; 2. likely, disposed, liable, prone, inclined; 3. bright, clever, alert, intelligent, receptive; *Ant.* 1. unfit, ill-becoming, unsuitable; 2. unlikely; 3. slow, retarded, dense.

***Argue*** : *vb.*1. debate, discuss; 2. dispute, diagree; *Ant.* 2. agree, concur.

***Argument*** : *n.* 1. discussion, debate, dispute, controversy, disagreement; 2. reason, ground, grounds, proof; *Ant.* agreement, harmony, accord.

***Aristocrat*** : *n.* nobleman, noble, peer, lord; *Ant.* commoner, peasant.

***Arouse*** : *vb.* awaken, stir, activate, animate, excite, stimulate, fire; *Ant.* calm, settle, soothe.

***Arrange*** : *vb.* 1. place, order, put in order, group, distribute, array; 2. organise, plan, prepare; *Ant.* 1. disarrange, disturb, disorder.

***Array*** : *vb.* 1. clothe, dress, attire; adorn, 2. arrange, order, line-up, distribute; *n.* 1. order, arrangement, line-up; 2. display, arrangement, exhibit; *Ant. n.* 1. disarray, disorder, disorganisation.

***Arrest*** : *vb.* 1. take into custody, seize, apprehend, catch, capture, take prisoner; 2. stop, check, stay, delay, hinder, slow; 3. attract, engage, capture; *n.* 1. seizure, capture, detention custody, apprehension, imprisonment; 2. halt, check, stoppage, delay, hindrance; *n.* phr. under arrest imprisoned, in custody, incarcerated; *Ant. vb.* 1. release, free; 2. activate, encourage, stimulate.

***Arrival*** : *n.* coming, advent; *Ant.* departure, leaving.

***Arrive*** : *vb.* 1. come, reach; 2. succeed, attain success; *Ant.* 1. leave, depart.

***Arrogance*** : *n.* insolence, pride, haughtiness; *Ant.* humility, humbleness, modesty.

***Arrogant*** : *adj.* proud, haughty, insolent, prideful, scornful; *Ant.* humble, modest.

***Artful*** : *adj.* tricky, cunning, clever, deceitful; *Ant.* artless.

***Artificial*** : *adj.* 1. unnatural, synthetic, man-made, manufactured, not genuine, unreal; 2. false, pretended, unnatural, feigned, fake, faked, fraudulent; *Ant.* real, genuine, authentic.

***Artless*** : *adj.* simple, naive, innocent, natural, open, frank, honest, sincere, candid, truthful; *Ant.* artful, sly.

***Ascend*** : *vb.* rise, mount, climb or go upward; *Ant.* descend.

***Ashamed*** : *adj* embarrassed, shamefaced, abashed, humiliated; *Ant.* proud.

***Ask*** : *vb.* 1. question, inquire of, seek information (from), put a question (to); 2. demand, request, charge, expect; 3. invite, call in; *Ant.* 1. answer, reply.

***Asleep*** : *adj.* sleeping, inactive, dormant; *Ant.* awake, alert.

***Assemble*** : *vb.* 1. meet, convene, collect, gather; 2. put together, connect, manufacture; *Ant.* 1. scatter, disperse 2. disassemble.

***Assent*** : *vb.* agree, consent (to); allow, concede, accede (to); *n.* consent, agreement, approval permission; *Ant. vb.* refuse deny, dissent, *n.* refusal denial.

***Assert*** : *vb.* 1. declare, state, affirm; 2. insit (on), emphasize, claim, support, uphold, maintain; *Ant.* 1. deny, contradict; 2. decline.

***Assertion*** : *n.* declaration, statement, affirmation; *Ant.* denial, contradiction.

***Assist*** : *vb.* aid, help, support, back; *Ant.* hinder, obstruct, impede, thwart.

***Assistance*** : *n.* help, aid, support; *Ant.* obstruction, interference.

***Associate*** : *vb.* 1. connect, relate, link; 2. join, ally, team up with, keep company (with), fraternise (with) father *n.* 1. companion, comrade, mate; 2. colleague, fellow. worker, partner, ally, confederate, accomplice; *Ant.* disassociate, disconnect.

***Assorted*** : *adj.* various varied, miscellaneous; *Ant.* same, alike.

***Assure*** : *vb.* pledge, promise. warrant, guarantee; *Ant.* deny, equivocate.

***Astonish*** : *vb.* surprise, amaze, astound, startle, shock, stupefy, stun; *Ant.* bore, tire.

***Attach*** : *vb.* 1. fasten, affix, fix, connect; 2. bind, tie, connect; *Ant.* 1. detach, unfasten, loosen, loose.

***Attachment*** : *n.* 1. devotion, regard, affection, fondness, liking; 2. fastening, tie, connection; *Ant.* detachment.

***Attack*** : *vb.* 1. assault, set upon, assail, charge, storm; 2. criticise, blame, abuse; charge, onslaught, encounter; *Ant. vb.* 1. withdraw, retreat; 2. praise, endorse. *n.* withdrawal, retreat.

***Attain*** : *vb.* accomplish, reach, achieve, gain, obtain, secure, procure, acquire, get; *Ant.* fail.

***Attainment*** : *n.* achievement, accomplishment; *Ant.* failure.

***Attempt*** : *vb.* try, seek; *n.* try, effort, undertaking, endeavour, trial; *Ant. vb.* achieve, accomplish. *n.* achievement, accomplishment.

***Attention*** : *n.* observation, heed, alertness, care, consideration; *Ant.* inattention, absent-mindedness, preoccupation.

***Attentive*** : *adj.* 1. observant, alert, heedful; 2. thoughtout, kind, polite, considerate, courteous; *Ant.* inattentive absentminded, preoccupied.

***Attract*** : *vb.* draw, invite, win; *Ant.* repel, repulse.

***Attractive*** : *adj.* appealing, alluring, pleasing, charming *Ant.* unattractive, plain, homely, ugly.

***Austere*** : *adj.* 1. stern, severe, hard, harsh, firm, strict, stiff, inflexible; 2. plain, simple, unadorned, severe; *Ant.* 1. lenient, permissive, soft; 2. luxurious, fancy, opulent.

***Austerity*** : *n.* severity, harshness, strictness; *Ant.* comfort, luxury.

***Authentic*** : *adj.* 1. genuine, real; 2. true, reliable, trustworthy, accurate, authoritative; *Ant.* fake, bogus, imitation, counterfeit.

***Authorise*** : *vb.* 1. empower; 2. allow, permit, sanction, approve; *Ant.* 2. prohibit, forbid.

***Automatic*** : *adj.* 1. self-moving, mechanical; 2. uncontrolled, uncontrollable, involuntary, unconscious; *Ant.* 1. manual, hand-operated; 2. deliberate, intentional.

***Available*** : *adj.* obtainable, accessible, at hand, ready, handy; *Ant.* unavailable, unobtainable.

***Average*** : *adj.* normal, common, typical, ordinary, mean, median *Ant. adj.* a typical, abnormal.

***Aversion*** : *n.* dislike, distaste, abhorrence, disgust, loathing, hatred; *Ant.* liking, affinity, attraction.

***Avoid*** : *vb.* elude, evade, shun; *Ant.* meet, confront, encounter, face.

***Aware*** : *adj.* conscious, informed, mindful; *Ant.* unaware, unconscious.

***Awe*** : *n.* respect, wonder, fear, admiration; *Ant.* scorn, contempt.

***Awful*** : *adj.* dreadful, terrible, abominable, bad, poor, unpleasant; *Ant.* wonderful delightful.

***Awkward*** : *adj.* 1. clumsy, graceless, unskillful, sloppy, ungraceful, ungainly, crude; 2. inconvenient, unwieldy, unmanageable; *Ant.* 1. graceful, deft, elegant, skilled, skillful.

# B

***Backward*** : *adv.* 1. rearward; 2. slow, underdeveloped, retarded; *Ant. adv.* forward, *adj.* 1. forward; 2. precious.

***Bad*** : *adj.* 1. evil, immoral, wicked, corrupt, sinful, depraved; 2. rotten, contaminated, spoiled, tainted; 3. harmful, injurious, unfavourable; 4. poor, defective, inferior, imperfect, substandard, faulty; 5. improper, inappropriate, unsuited, unsuitable; 6. upset, sorry; 7. sick, ill, out of sorts, suffering; 8. disagreeable, unpleasant, uncomfortable; 9. cross, nasty, unpleasant, unfriendly, irritable, disagreeable, irascible, short-tempered; *Ant.* good.

***Baffle*** : *vb.* mystify, puzzle, bewilder; *Ant.* enlighten, inform.

***Balloon*** : *vb.* swell, enlarge, put up or out; *Ant.* shrink, shrivel.

***Balmy*** : *adj.* mild, gentle, soothing; *Ant.* stormy, tempestuous. *ban vb.* forbid, prohibit, disallow, outlaw; *n.* prohibition, taboo; *Ant. vb.* permit, allow.

***Banish*** : *vb.* exile, deport, expel, dismiss; *Ant.* embrace, receive, admit, welcome.

***Bar*** : *n.* 1. barrier, obstacle, barricade, obstruction, hindrance, impediment; 2. counter, saloon, cocktail longue, cafe; *vb.* prevent, obstruct, hinder, impede, stop, deter, prohibit, block; *Ant. n.* 1. encouragement, aid; *vb.* permit, allow.

***Barbarian*** : *n.* savage, brute, boor, ruffian; *adj.*savage, rude, primitive, uncivilised, uncultured, crude, barbaric, barbarous; *Ant. adj.*cultivated, civilised, polished, sophistriated, square, tasteful.

***Bare*** : *adj.* 1. nude, naked, unclothed, uncovered, undressed; 2. plain, unfurnished, empty, barren; 3. mere, scarce; *vb.*reveal, disclose, expose, publicise; *Ant. adj.*1. clothed, dressed, garbed, *vb.*hide, conceal, disguise.

***Barren*** : *adj.* sterile, unproductive, unfruitful, bare, childless; *Ant.* fertile, fruitful.

***Barricade*** : *n.* barrier, obstruction, fence, enclosure; *vb.* shut in obstruct, block, bar; *Ant. vb.*release, free, open.

***Barrier*** : *n.* 1. bar, barricade, fence, wall, railing, obstacle; 2. obstruction, hindrance, impediment, restraint, obstacle, limit; *Ant.* 2. encouragement, aid, assistance.

***Base***[1] : *n.* bottom, support, stand, rest, foundation; *vb.* found, establish; *Ant. n.* top, peak, pinnacle.

***Base***[2] : *adj.* 1. low, immoral, bad, evil, depraved, wicked, mean, selfish; 2. cheap, tawdry, worthless, poor, debased (of coin) counterfeit; *Ant.* 1. noble, exalted, virtuous; 2. refined, valuable.

***Bashful*** : *adj.* shy, timid, sheepish, modest, coy, shamefaced, ashamed; *Ant.* self-assured, immodest, arrogant.

***Basic*** : *adj.* main, chief, essential, fundamental; *Ant.* subordinate, subsidiary.

***Beautiful*** : *adj.* pretty, lovely, handsome, attractive; *Ant.* homely, unattractive, plain, ugly.

***Beauty*** : *n.* loveliness, comeliness, attractiveness; *Ant.* homeliness, plainness, ugliness.

***Begin*** : *vb.* 1. start, commence, initiate, inaugurate; 2. originate, create, arise; *Ant.* 1. stop, end, finish, terminate.

***Beginner*** : *n.* amateur, non-professional, apprentice; *Ant.* professional.

***Beginning*** : *n.* 1. start, outset, commencement, emergence, initiation, inauguration; 2. origin, source, rise, birth, creation; *Ant.* ending, finish termination.

***Behave*** : *vb.* act, conduct, oneself, deport oneself; *Ant.* misbehave, rebel.

***Behaviour*** : *n.* conduct, deportment, manners; *Ant.* misbehaviour, rebelliousness.

***Bend*** : *vb.* 1. curve, bow, deflect; 2. stoop, kneel, crouch, bow; 3. submit, yield, bow, stoop, agree; 4. subdue, suppress, oppress, influence, cause to yield, submit, or bow; *Ant.* 1. straighten.

***Beneficial*** : *adj.* good, advantageous, helpful, useful, profitable, wholesome; *Ant.* unwholesome, disadvantageous.

***Benefit*** : *n.* service, favour, help, support, good, profit, advantage; *vb.* help, aid, support, profit, serve; *Ant.n.* disadvantage.

***Benevolent*** : *adj.* humane, good, kind, well-wishing, kindly, kind-hearted, well-disposed, generous, open-hearted, liberal, charitable; *Ant.* malevolent, mean, cruel, evil.

***Bent*** : *adj.* 1. crooked, curved; 2. determined, resolved, set, decided, firm; *Ant.* 1. straight.

***Bestow*** : *vb.* give, confer, present, award; *Ant.* withhold, withdraw.

***Betray*** : *vb.* 1. deliver, be treacherous or disloyal; 2. reveal, expose; display, show, exhibit; *Ant.* safeguard, protect, shelter.

***Better*** : *vb.* improve; *Ant.* worsen.

***Bewilder*** : *vb.* confuse, puzzle, perplex, mystify, overwhelm; *Ant.* enlighten , clarify.

***Bias*** : *n.* prejudice, tendency, inclination; *vb.* influence, prejudice, bend;'*Ant. n.* impartiality, fairness.

***Bind*** : *vb.* 1. tie, fasten, band; 2. obligate, oblige; *Ant.* 1. loosen, free, untie.

***Bitter*** : *adj.* 1. acrid, harsh, biting; 2. distressing, distressful, painful, grievous; 3. painful, stinging, piercing, biting; 4. hostile, hated, severe, vicious; *Ant.* 1. sweet, bland.

***Black*** : *adj.* 1. dark, sooty, inky, ebon, swarthy; 2. soiled, dirty, filthy, stained; 3. gloomy, dismal, sad, depressing, dark, *Ant.* 1. white, light-skinned; 2. clean, pure, pristine;, 3. bright, cheerful.

***Blame*** : *vb.* reproach, condemn, criticise; *n.* responsibility, guilt, fault; *Ant.* honour, credit.

***Blank*** : *adj.* 1. empty, unmarked; 2. uninterested, expressionless; *n.* void, area, form, vacancy; *Ant. adj.* 1. filled. 2. animated, alert.

***Blaze*** : *n.* flame, fire, holocaust, inferno; *vb.* burn, flare, flare up, flame, shine; *Ant. vb.* dwindle, die.

***Bleach*** : *vb.* whiten, blanch, pale; *n.* whitener; *Ant. vb.* darken, blacken.

***Bleak*** : *adj.* 1. bare, desolate, barren, windswept; 2. depressing, cheerless, gloomy, dreary; *Ant.* 2. hopeful, cheerful, promising.

***Blend*** : *vb.* mix, intermix, intermingle, mingle, commingle, combine; *mixture* combination, compound; *vb.* separate, divide.

***Bliss*** : *n.* happiness, joy, gladness, ecstasy, rapture; *Ant.* misery, unhappiness, torment.

***Bloody*** : *adj.* bloodthirsty, cruel, inhuman, pitiless, ruthless, murderous, ferocious; *Ant.* gentle, kind.

***Bloom*** : *n.* flower, blossom; *Ant.* vb. wither, shrivel.

***Blossom*** : *n.* flower, bloom; *vb.* bloom, flower, flourish; *Ant.* *vb.*wither, shrink, dwindle, fade.

***Blue*** : *n.* azure, sapphire; *adj.* sad, gloomy, depressed, unhappy, dejected, melancholy; *Ant.* *adj.* happy, cheerful, optimistic.

***Blunt*** : *adj.* 1. dull, unsharpened, rounded, worn; 2. rude, crude, direct, impolite, abrupt, short, curt, brusque, gruff; *vb.* dull; *Ant.* *adj.*1. sharp, keen, pointed 2. diplomatic, tactful.

***Blur*** : *vb.* stain, sully, obscure, dim, dull, confuse; *n.* smudge, smear, stain, spot; *Ant.* *vb.* clarify, clear.

***Bold*** : *adj.* 1. brave, unafraid, fearless, intrepid, courageous, daring, valiant, heroic, gallant; 2. rude, disrespectful, insolent, impudent, shameless; *Ant.* 1. cowardly, fearful, timid, timorous. 2. courteous, polite, deferential.

***Boom*** : *vb.* 1. reverberate, thunder, roar; 2. prosper, flourish *n.*1. blast, roar, thunder; 2. prosperity, rush *Ant.* *n.*2. recession.

***Border*** : *n.* 1. frontier, boundary, limit; 2. edge, margin; *vb.* join, adjoin, edge, abut; *Ant.* *n.* 2. center, middle.

***Bore*** : *vb.* 1. weary, tire; 2. drill, hole, perforate; *Ant.* 1. interest, excite, arouse, captivate.

***Boss*** : *n.* manager, director, supervisor, employer, foreman; *Ant.* employee, worker, underling.

***Bother*** : *vb.* irritate, trouble, worry, disturb, annoy, vex, pester, upset, inconvenience; *n.* trouble, inconvenience, upset, distress, anxiety; *Ant.* *n.* comfort, solace.

***Bottom*** : *n.*1. base, foot, depths; 2. underside; 3. seat, buttocks, behind, rear; *Ant.*1.,2. top, topside.

***Bound*** : *adj.* 1. tied, trussed, shackled, fettered; 2. sure, certain, destined, required compelled; *Ant.* 1. unfettered, free.

***Bourgeois*** : *adj.* middle-class, commonplace, ordinary, common, conventional; *Ant.* aristocratic, upperclass.

***Boy*** : *n.* lad, youth, youngster, kid; *Ant.* man, girl.

***Brag*** : *vb.* boast, swagger; *Ant.* deprecate, depreciate.

***Brain*** : *n.* (usually brains) intelligence, sense, commonsense, intellect, reason, understanding; *Ant.* stupidity.

***Brave*** : *adj.* courageous, gallant, fearless, daring, valiant valorous, intrepid, unafraid, heroic, bold; *Ant.* timid, cowardly, fearful, craven.

***Bravery*** : *n.* courage, daring, valour, fearlessness, heroism, boldness; *Ant.* cowardice, timidity, fearfulness.

***Brazen*** : *adj.* bold, brassy, shamelessness, impudent, insolent, rude, immodest; *Ant.* modest, retiring, shy, self-effacing.

***Breach*** : *n.* 1. break, rift, rupture, fracture, crack, opening, gap; 2. violation, breaking; *Ant.* 2. observation.

***Break*** : *vb.* 1. fracture, rupture, shatter, smash, wreck, crash, atomise, demolish; 2. violate, disobey; 3. disintegrate, fall apart, collapse, splinter, smash, shatter; *n.* 1. crack, gap, opening, breach, rupture; 2. suspension, stop, hesitation, interruption; *Ant. vb.* 1. mend, repair, 2. obey.

***Breeze*** : *n.* breath, air, zephyr, wind; *Ant.* calm.

***Bridle*** : *n.* curb, check, restraint, control, halter, hackamore; *vb.* curb, control, check, restrain, govern; *Ant. vb.* loose, free, release.

***Brief*** : *adj.* 1. short, temporary, fleeting; 2. short, terse, concise, condensed, compact; *vb.* advise, teach, instruct; *Ant. adj.* 1. long, extended, protracted; 2. extensive, comprehensive, exhaustive.

***Bright*** : *adj.* 1. shining, shiny, gleaming, brilliant, sparkling, shimmering, radiant; 2. lively, cheerful, happy, gay, lighthearted; 3. vivid, brilliant; 4. intelligent, quick-witted, clever, keen; 5. promising, encouraging, favourable; *Ant.* 1. dull, dim, lustreless; 2. boring, dull, colourless; 4. stupid, slow, backward.

***Brilliant*** : *adj.* 1. bright, splendid, radiant, shining, sparkling, glittering; 2. talented, intelligent, gifted, ingenious; *Ant.* 1. dull, lustreless; 2. mediocre, second-rate.

***Brim*** : *n.* edge, lip, rim, margin, border; *Ant.* centre, middle.

***Bring*** : *vb.* carry, take fetch; *Ant. vb.* withdraw, remove.

***Brisk*** : *adj.* 1. lively, active, animated, energetic, nimble, quick, agile, spry; 2. sharp, cool, stimulating, keen, invigorating; *Ant.* 1. slow, sluggish, lethargic; 2. heavy, still, oppressive.

***Brittle*** : *adj.* frail, fragile, breakable, weak; *Ant.* flexible, elastic, supple.

***Broad*** : *adj.* 1. wide, large, expansive, extended, roomy; 2. general; 3. extensive, wide, full; *Ant.* 1. narrow, constricted; 3. limited, negligible.

***Broad-minded*** : *adj.* tolerant, open-minded, unprejudiced, unbigotted, liberal; *Ant.* narrow-minded, prejudiced, bigotted, petty.

***Brutal*** : *adj.* cruel, mean, savage, pitiless, inhuman, barbaric, ferocious; *Ant.* kind, kindhearted, gentle, mild.

***Build*** : *vb.* construct, erect, put together, assemble; *n.* physique. *Ant. vb.* demolish, raze.

***Bulge*** : *n.* swelling, lump, protrusion, protuberance, bump; *vb.* swell, protrude, extend; *Ant. n.* depression, hollow.

***Bulky*** : *adj.* large, big, huge, clumsy, unwieldy, cumbersome, massive; *Ant.* delicate, small, handy.

***Burst*** : *vb.* explode, blow up, erupt; *Ant.* implode.

***Bury*** : *vb.* 1. inter, entomb; 2. hide, conceal, cover, secrete; *Ant.* disinter, raise.

***Busy*** : *adj.* active, occupied, engaged, employed, industrious, hardworking; *Ant.* inactive, unemployed, indolent, lazy.

***Buy*** : *vb.* purchase, procure, obtain, get; *Ant.* sell.

# C

***Cagey*** : *adj.* tricky, cunning, clever, cautious, wary, shrewd, evasive; *Ant.* guileless, innocent, naive, straightforward.

***Calamity*** : *n.* bad luck, misfortune, distress, trouble, hardship, reverse, catastrophe; *Ant.* boon, blessing.

***Calculate*** : *vb.* 1. figure, reckon, compute, tally, measure, determine, add, subtract, multiply, divide; 2. estimate, judge, deliberate; *Ant.* 1. guess, assume.

***Calculating*** : *adj.* scheming, crafty, cunning, shrewd; *Ant.* ingenuous, simple, direct, guileless.

***Calculation*** : *n.* computation, figuring, estimation, reckoning; *Ant.* assumption, guess.

***Calm*** : *adj.* 1. quiet, peaceful, still, tranquil, mild, serene, smooth; 2. serene, cool, composed, collected, unruffled, level-headed, unexcited, detached, aloof; *n.* calmness, stillness, serenity, quiet, composure; *vb.* pacify, tranquillise, soothe; *Ant. adj.* 1. tempestuous, roiled, disturbed. 2. emotional, disturbed, excited; *n.* turmoil, upheaval, disturbance; *vb.* upset, excite, disturb.

***Cancel*** : *vb.* 1. delete, cross out *or* off, erase; 2. call off, void, rescind, set aside, recall; *Ant.* 2. ratify.

**Capable** : *adj.* able, skilled, fit, skillful, accomplished, competent; *Ant.* inept, incompetent, unskilled.

**Capacity** : *n.* 1. volume, content; 2. ability, capability, aptitude, talent, faculty; *Ant.* 2. incapacity, inability.

**Capital** : *n.* cash, money, assets, property, wealth, principal, resources; *adj.* major, chief, first, primary, leading, important, principal; *Ant. adj.* trivial, unimportant, secondary.

**Captivity** : *n.* imprisonment, confinement, detention, custody; slavery, bondage; *Ant.* freedom, liberty.

**Capture** : *vb.* seize, take prisoner, trap, grab, nab, catch, arrest; *n.* seizure, catching, recovery; *Ant. vb.* release, free, liberate.

**Cardinal** :*adj.* important, chief, principal, primary, prime, major, leading, essential; *Ant.* secondary, subordinate, auxiliary.

**Care** : *n.* 1. worry, concern, anxiety, trouble; 2. carefulness, attention, regard, concern, consideration; 3. charge, custody, protection, keeping, supervision, guardianship; *vb.* 1. attend, consider regard; 2. watch, guard, keep, supervise; *Ant. n.* 2. indifference, unconcern.

**Careful** : *adj.* 1. cautious, watchful, wary, guarded, vigilant; 2. thorough, concerned, painstaking, meticulous; *Ant.* 1. incautious, heedless; 2. carefless, messy, sloppy.

**Careless** : *adj.* messy, unthoughtful, unconcerned, negligent, reckless, thoughtless, uncaring; *Ant.* careful, cautious, prudent, painstaking.

**Casual** : *adj.* 1. chance, accidental, unintentional, unexpected, offhand, unplanned, spontaneous; 2. informal, sport, sporty; *Ant.* 1. planned, calculated, deliberate, premeditated; 2. formal, dressy.

**Catastrophe** : *n.* disaster, calamity, accident, misfortune, mishap; *Ant.* boon, blessing, triumph.

***Catch*** : *vb.* 1. seize, capture, take, grasp, grab, nab; 2. hook, trap, snare, entrap, ensnare; *Ant. vb.* 1., 2. release, free.

***Caution*** : *n.* 1. wariness, watchfulness, vigilance, heed, care; 2. warning, advice; *vb.* warn, admonish, forewarn; *Ant. n.* 1. headlessness, carelessness, incaution.

***Cautious*** : *adj.* careful, watchful, wary, vigilant; *Ant.* heedless, headstrong, indiscreet, foolish.

***Cease*** : *vb.* stop, end, put a stop or an end to, terminate; *Ant.* begin, start.

***Celebrate*** : *vb.* honour, observe, keep, commemorate; *Ant.* ignore, disregard.

***Celebrated*** : *adj.* famous, renowned, famed, well-known, noted, illustrious, eminent, popular; *Ant.* anonymous, unknown.

***Cenure*** : *n.* disapproval, criticism, reproach; *vb.* disapprove, criticise condemn, reproach; *Ant. n.* approval, praise; *vb.* praise, approve, applaud.

***Centre*** : *n.* 1. middle, midst, inside, midpoint; 2. focus, hub, heart, core; *vb.* focus, direct, concentrate; *Ant. n.* 1. edge, brim.

***Central*** : *adj.* 1. middle, mid, focal, inner, halfway; 2. principal, chief, dominant, basic, fundamental, necessary; *Ant.* 2. secondary, auxiliary, side, incidental.

***Certain*** : *adj.* 1. confident, sure, positive, assured; 2. definite, particular, special; *Ant.* 1. doubtful, uncertain, questionable.

***Certainly*** : *adv.* surely, absolutely, definitely; *Ant.* doubtfully, doubiously, questionably.

***Chance*** : *n.* 1. opportunity, possibility, prospect; 2. luck, accident, fate; *adj.* accidental, casual; *Ant. n.* 2. certainty, inevitability.

**Change** : *vb.* 1. exchange, substitute, replace; 2. vary, modify, alter; 3. exchange, trade; *n.* variation, modification, alteration; *Ant. vb.* endure, remain; *n.* endurance, steadfastness, immutability.

**Chaos** : *n.* disorder, confusion, turmoil; *Ant.* tranquillity, order, organisation, tidiness.

**Chaotic** : *adj.* disordered, confused, messy, disorganised; *Ant.* ordered, organised, neat, systematic.

**Charitable** : *adj.* kind, generous, liberal; considerate; *Ant.* mean, petty, stingy, narrow-minded.

**Chaste** : *adj.* virtuous, pure, innocent, decent, virginal; *Ant.* impure, worldly, sinful, immodest.

**Cheap** : *adj.* 1. inexpensive, low-priced, low-cost; 2. shoddy, inferior, poor; *Ant.* 1. costly, expensive, dear; 2. elegant, well-made.

**Check** : *vb.* 1. stop, halt, arrest, block; 2. control, curb, hinder; 3. review, investigate, test, examine, compare; *n.* 1. control, curb, hindrance, barrier, bar, obstacle, restriction; 2. stub, counterfoil, ticket, coupon, receipt; *Ant. vb.* 1., 2. advance, continue, foster, promote.

**Cheer** : *n.* 1. approval, applause, encouragement; 2. glee, joy, mirth, gaiety, cheerfulness; *vb.* 1. gladden, encourage, comfort; 2. shout, yell, applaud; Ant *n.* 1. discouragement, derision; *vb.* 1. discourage, sadden; 2. boo, hiss.

**Cheerful** : *adj.* cheery, happy, joyous, joyful, gay, merry; *Ant.* sad, gloomy, morose, downhearted.

**Cherish** : *vb.* 1. nurse, comfort, nurture; 2. treasure, hold dear, value, prize; *Ant.* 2 scorn, undervalue, depreciate, disparage.

**Chide** : *vb.* scold, criticise, admonish, reprimand, rebuke, reprove; *Ant.* praise, extol, commend.

**Chief** : *n.* leader, ruler, commander, boss, head; *adj.* leading, principal, main head; *adj.* secondary, incidental, auxiliary, accidental, chiefly; *adv.* mostly, mainly, principally, especially; *Ant.* lastly, last.

***Childish*** : *adj.* childlike, immature, babyish, infantile; *Ant.* adult, grown-up, mature, seasoned.

***Chill*** : *n.* cold, coldness, coolness, cool; *adj.* chilly, cool, brisk, frosty; *Ant. n.* warmth, heat. *adj.* warm, heated, hot.

***Chivalrous*** : *adj.* brave, valorous, noble, polite, courteous, gallant, gentlemanly; *Ant.* rude, impolite, crude, uncivil.

***Chronic*** : *adj.* continuing, persistent, continuous, lingering, perennial, sustained, constant, lifelong, permanent, unending, eternal, everlasting; *Ant.* acute, fleeting, temporary.

***Civil*** : *adj.* 1. municipal, public; 2. polite, courteous, respectful, gracious, well-mannered; *Ant.* 2. impolite, rude, crude.

***Clamour*** : *n.* din, noise, shouting, uproar; *vb.* demand noisily, shout; *Ant. n.* quiet, serenity, tranquillity.

***Clarify*** : *vb.* explain, clear, define *Ant.* confuse, muddle, obscure.

***Clash*** : *n.* clang, crash, clank; 2. conflict, opposition, struggle, disagreement, collision; *vb.* 1. contrast, mismatch, conflict. 2. contend, conflict, disagree, interfere, collide; *n.* 2. harmony, agreement, accord. *vb.* harmonise, blend; 2. agree, match.

***Clean*** : *adj.* 1. neat, tidy, clear, dustless, immaculate, unsoiled, unstained. 2. pure, untained, uncontaminated, purified. *vb.* 1. dust, mop, vacuum, scour, scrub, sweep, wipe, wash, rinse, cleanse; 2. purify, decontaminate, sterilise; *Ant. adj.* dirty, soiled, impure, contaminated. *vb.* soil, dirty, pollute.

***Clear*** : *adj.* 1. plain, understandable, district, lucid, obvious. 2. uncludly unclouded, bright, light; sunny, fair; 3. certain, sure, doubtless, obvious; 4. open, free, unobstructed, unblocked; *vb.* 1. empty. 2. acquit, free, release, emancipate, let go; 3. rid, loose, unloose, free, remove; *Ant. adj.* 1. confused, muddled; 2. overcast, cludy, dark; 3. dubious, questionable; 4. obstructed, blocked, blockaded; *vb.* 1. fill, clutter. 2. implicate, involve; 3. obstruct, block, blockade.

***Clearly*** : *adv.* obviously, definitely, plainly, evidently, unmistakably, certainly, surely; *Ant.* dubiously, questionably.

***Clever*** : *adj.* 1. bright, intelligent, shrewd, quick, talented, expert, gifted, smart; 2. skillful, adroit, dexterous, handy; *Ant.* 1. stupid, slow, backward, dull; 2. clumsy, maladroit, inept.

***Climb*** : *vb.* scale, ascend, mount; *Ant.* descend.

***Cloak*** : *n.* cape, mantle, wrap, shawl; *vb.* conceal, hide, cover, mask; *Ant. vb.* reveal, show, display.

***Close***[1] : *vb.* 1. shut, fasten, bolt, lock; 2. end, terminate, conclude; *Ant.* 1. open, unlock; 2. begin, start.

***Close***[2] : *adj.* 1. near, nearby; 2. stuffy, unventilated, oppressive; 3. stingy, mean, mingy, tight; *Ant.* 1. far, distant; 2. fresh, clear; 3. generous, open-handed, charitable.

***Cloudy*** : *adj.* 1. dim, obscure, vague, indefinite, blurred, unclear, confused; 2. overcast, clouded, sunless, gloomy; *Ant.* 1. clearheaded, lucid, clarified; 2. sunny, clear, brilliant, cloudless.

***Clumsy*** : *adj.* awkward, ungraceful, unskillful, bungling, bumbling, ungainly, inept; *Ant.* graceful, adroit, skillful, polished, dexterous.

***Coarse*** : *adj.* rough, crude rude; *Ant.* fine, refined, cultivated, genteel, suave.

***Coax*** : *vb.* wheedle, persuade, cajole, urge; *Ant.* bully, force, coerce.

***Cold*** : *adj.* 1. cool, chilly, chill, frigid, freezing; 2. cool, chilly, unemotional, unfriendly, unfeeling, indifferent, heartless; *Ant.* 1. hot, warm, temperate, 2. friendly, warm, compassionate, outgoing.

***Collect*** : *vb.*1. gather, assemble, accumulate; 2. solicit, obtain, procure, secure, get raise; *Ant.* 1. disperse, dispel, scatter.

***Colossal*** : *adj.* enormous, huge, immense, gigantic; *Ant.* tiny, miniature, minuscule, microscopic.

***Combet*** : *vb.* fight, battle, oppose, contest, struggle *n.* fight, battle, contest, conflict, war, struggle; *Ant. vb.* surrender, yield, succumb.

***Combination*** : *n.* 1. blending mixing, compounding; 2. blend, mixture, compound, composite; *Ant.* 1. separation, division.

***Combine*** : *vb.* blend, mix, unite, join, connect; *Ant.* separate, divide.

***Come*** : *vb.* 1. approach, advance, near; 2. arrive, reach; *Ant.* go, leave, depart.

***Ccomfort*** : *vb.* soothe, relieve, console, ease, calm, cheer; *n.* 1 solace, consolation; 2. relaxation, rest, satisfaction, luxury, case; *Ant. vb.* upset, agitate, disturb, discompose, *n.* 1. uncertainty. 2. discomfort.

***Comfortable*** : *adj.* 1. relaxed, easy, rested, contented, cheerful; restful, cozy, satisfying; *Ant.* 1. uncomfortable, strained, tense, edgy.

***Command*** : *vb.* order, direct, demand, decree, rule; *n.*order, demand, direction, rule, decree, charge, authority; *Ant. vb.*obey.

***Commence*** : *vb.* begin, start, open; *Ant.* end, stop, terminate, finish.

***Commend*** : *vb.* praise, recommend, applaud, laud; *Ant.* blame, censure, criticise.

***Commendable*** : *adj.* praiseworthy, deserving; *Ant.* deplorable, bad, lamentable.

***Commendation*** : *n.* praise, approval, recommendation, applause, medal, honour; *Ant.* condemnation, criticism, censure.

***Common*** : *adj.* joint, communal, mutual, shared; 2. customary, usual, regular; 3. ordinary, natural, conventional, plain, commonplace, stale, trite; 4. ordinary coarse, vulgar, low; *Ant.* 1. separate, different. 2. unusual, rare; 3. distinctive, outstanding, extraordinary; 4. refined, cultivated, genteel.

***Commonplace*** : *adj.* ordinary, common, everyday, usual, undistinguished, frequent, run-of-the-mill; *Ant.* unusual, distinctive, original.

***Communicate*** : *vb.* 1. impart, convey, transmit, reveal, disclose, divulge, advertise, publicise, publish; 2. transmit; *Ant.* 1. conceal, withhold, dissemble.

***Compact*** : *adj.* compressed, packed, tight, thick; *n.* 1. makeup box or case, vanity; 2. agreement, treaty, contract, pact, convenant; *Ant. adj.* loose, unconfined, sprawling, unfettered.

***Competence*** : *n.* ability, skill, capability; *Ant.* incompetence, ineptitude.

***Competent*** : *adj.* capable, skillful, qualified, apt, able, proficient; *Ant.* incompetent, inept, awkward, gauche.

***Competitor*** : *n.* contestant, rival, opponent; *Ant.* friend, ally, colleague.

***Complete*** : *adj.* 1. whole, full, entire; 2. ended, over, finished, done, concluded; *vb.* finish, end, conclude, terminate, close; *Ant. adj.* unfinished, incomplete, partial; *vb.* begin, start, commence.

***Complex*** : *adj.* complicated, involved, intricate; *Ant.* simple, uncomplicated, rudimentary.

***Compliment*** : *n.* praise, honour, admiration, approval, commendation, appreciation; *vb.* praise, honour, approve, commend, flatter; *Ant. n.* insult, aspersion, affront; *vb.* insult, affront, disparage.

***Composed*** : *adj.* relaxed, calm, cool, untroubled, peaceful, serene, tranquil, quiet; *Ant.* agitated, nervous, anxious, overwrought, hysterical.

***Compound*** : *n.* mixture, combination, aggregate; *adj.* complicated, complex, combined, mixed; *Ant. adj.* simple, uncomplicated.

***Comprehensive*** : *adj.* inclusive, broad, wide, complete, full; *Ant.* partial, fragmentary, incomplete, limited.

***Compress*** : *vb.* squeeze, compact, press, crowd, pack; *Ant.* stretch, spread, expand.

***Compulsory*** : *adj.* necessary, required, unavoidable, obligatory; *Ant.* optional, elective, unrestricted, free.

***Conceal*** : *vb.* hide, cover, secrete; *Ant.* reveal, show, display, expose.

***Concede*** : *vb.* admit, allow, acknowledge, yield; *Ant.* deny, contradict, negate.

***Conceit*** : *n.* vanity, egotism, self-esteem; *Ant.* modesty, humility, humbleness, self-effacement.

***Conceited*** : *adj.* vain, arrogant, proud, smug, self-important, egotistical; *Ant.* modest, humble, self-effacing.

***Concentrate*** : *vb.* 1. focus, localise, condense; 2. ponder, centre, meditate, scrutinise; *Ant.* 1. diffuse, scatter, disperse, dissipate.

***Concentration*** : *n.* application, study, attention; *Ant.* distraction, confusion.

***Concern*** : *vb.* 1. interest, relate to, affect, touch, involve; 2. worry, trouble, disturb; *n.* 1. interest, consequences; 2. anxiety, worry, care; 3. business, firm, company, house, partnership corporation; *Ant. vb.* 1. disinterest, bore, tire; 2. soothe, calm; *n.* 1. 2. disinterest, indifference.

***Concerted*** : *adj.* joint, united, combined; *Ant.* unorganised, individual, separate.

***Concession*** : *n.* yielding, admission, granting; *Ant.* demand, insistence.

***Conclude*** : *vb.* 1. finish, end, terminate, complete; 2. arrange, settle, determine, decide; 3. presume, assume, gather, understand, deduce; *Ant.* 1. begin, start, commence.

***Conclusion*** : *n.* end, finish, termination, close; *Ant.* beginning, start, opening, commencement.

***Concrete*** : *adj.* firm, definite, solid, precise; *Ant.* vague, undetermined, amorphous.

***Condemn*** : *vb.* 1. denounce, rebuke, blame; 2. judge, doom, punish, convict, sentence; *Ant.* 1. praise, laud, extol, applaud; 2. pardon, absolve, excuse.

***Condense*** : *vb.* reduce, abbreviate, shorten, abridge, concentrate, compress, digest, diminish; *Ant.* expand, enlarge, swell, increase.

***Confer*** : *vb.* 1. give, award, bestow, grant; 2. discuss, consult, deliberate; *Ant.* 1. withdraw, retrieve.

***Confidence*** : *n.* 1. trust, faith, reliance; 2. self-assurance, self-reliance, self-confidence, courage; *Ant.* 1. distrust, mistrust, doubt; 2. shyness, modesty, diffidence.

***Confident*** : *adj.* sure, certain, self-assured, self-reliant, self-confident, dauntless; *Ant.* timid, uncertain, shy, self-effacing.

***Confine*** : *vb.* limit, restrict, bound, hinder; *Ant.* release, free.

***Confirm*** : *vb.* 1. assure, verify, corroborate, substantiate; 2. validate, approve, ratify; *Ant.* 1. deny, disclaim, disavow.

***Confirmed*** : *adj.* habitual, established, chronic, regular; *Ant.* infrequent, occasional.

***Conflict*** : *vb.* oppose, clash, contend; *n.* 1. fight, battle, struggle, encounter, engagement; 2. controversy, disagreement, contest; *Ant. vb.* agree, harmonise, concur, coincide; *n.* agreement, harmony, concurrence.

***Conform*** : *vb.* comply, submit, yield, obey; 2. agree, correspond, *Ant.* 1. rebel. 2. disagree, vary.

***Confuse*** : *vb.* 1. puzzle, perplex, bewilder, mystify, baffle, mislead; 2. mistake, mix up, jumble; *Ant.* 1. enlighten, edify, illuminate, clarify. 2. differentiate, distinguish.

***Confusion*** : *n.* 1. perlexity, bewilderment, uncertainty; 2. disorder, mess, muss, turmoil, upset; *Ant.* 1. enlightenment, understanding, comprehension. 2. organisation, tidiness.

***Congregate*** : *vb.* meet, gather, convene, foregather; *Ant.* disperse, scatter, dissipate, dispel.

***Conjunction*** : *n.* junction, link, combination, connection; *Ant.* disconnection, separation, diversion.

***Connect*** : *vb.* 1. unite, join, link, combine; 2. associate, relate; *Ant.* 1. disconnect, disjoin; 2. dissociate, disasociate.

***Connection*** : *n.* 1. junction, union, link, bond, tie; 2. association, relationship, bond, tie; *Ant.* 2. dissociation, disassociation.

***Conquer*** : *vb.* 1. succeed, win, gain, achieve; 2. defeat, overcome, overpower, subdue; *Ant.* 2. surrender, yield.

***Conquest*** : *n.* triumph, victory; *Ant.* failure, surrender.

***Conscientious*** : *adj.* honest, upright, scrupulous, straight, straightforward, incorruptible; *Ant.* irresponsible, careless, slovenly.

***Conscious*** : *adj.* 1. aware; 2. awake, sensible; 3. deliberate, intentional, purposeful; *Ant.* unaware, insensitive, 2. asleep, insensible, comatose; 3. careless, indifferent, slack, negligent.

***Consent*** : *vb.* agree, permit, allow, let, assent; *n.* permission, agreement, assent; Ant *vb.* refuse, dissent. *n.* refusal, dissent.

***Consequence*** : *n.* 1. result, outcome, effect, issue; *Ant.* cause, impetus.

***Conservative*** : *adj.* 1. reactionary, right-wing, conventional; 2. moderate, cautious, careful; *Ant.* 1. liberal, radical; 2. reckless, rash, adventurous, foolhardy.

***Conserve*** : *vb.* preserve, keep, retain; *Ant.* squander, waste, use.

***Consider*** : *vb.* 1. study, think about, deliberate, reflect on, contemplate; 2. think of, regard, look upon, judge, estimate; *Ant.* 1. ignore, disregard, disdain.

***Considerate*** : *adj.* kind, thoughtful, polite; *Ant.* inconsiderate, thoughtless, selfish.

***Consistent*** : *adj.* 1. agreeing, compatible, harmonious; 2. regular, expected, faithful; *Ant.* 1. contrary, opposed, antagonistic. 2. inconsistent, erratic, eccentric.

***Consolation*** : *n.* solace, comfort, sympathy; *Ant.* discouragement, discomfort, burden.

***Console*** : *vb.* solace, comfort, sympathise with; *Ant.* disturb, upset.

***Conspicuous*** : *adj.* noticeable, visible, clear, prominent, obvious, outstanding; *Ant.* inconspicuous, neutral.

***Constant*** : *adj.* 1. unchanging, fixed, stable, invariable, unchangeable; 2. loyal, faithful, steadfast, true, staunch, devoted, steady, firm; *Ant.* 1. irregular, off-and-on, periodic. 2. occasional, infrequent.

***Construct*** : *vb.* build, erect, raise; *Ant.* destroy, demolish, raze.

***Constructive*** : *adj.* helpful, useful, valuable; *Ant.* destructive, ruinous.

***Contemplative*** : *adj.* thoughtful, meditative, studious, pensive; *Ant.* indifferent, inattentive, thoughtless.

***Contemporary*** : *adj.* 1. contemporaneous, simultaneous, coexisting, coexistent; 2. modern, up-to-date, fashionable; *Ant.* 1. antecedent, succeeding.

***Contempt*** : *n.* scorn, disdain, malice; *Ant.* admiration, approbation.

***Contemptible*** : *adj.* low, base, mean, detestable, miserable; *Ant.* admirable, honourable.

***Contemptuous*** : *adj.* scornful, disdainful, insolent, sneering; *Ant.* humble, modest, self-effacing.

***Content*** : *adj.* happy, satisfied, pleased, contented; *Ant.* dissatisfied, restless, discontented.

***Continual*** : *adj.* regular, consecutive, connected; *Ant.* irregular, intermittent, occasional.

***Continue*** : *vb.* 1. persist; 2. proceed, resume, recommence, renew; 3. endure, last, remain, stay; *Ant.* discontinue, stop, cease, interrupt.

***Continuous*** : *adj.* uniterrupted, continuing, ceaseless, incessant, unceasing, constant, unending; *Ant.* irregular, intermittent, sporadic.

***Contract*** : 2. diminish, reduce, condense, shrink; *Ant. vb.* expand, swell, enlarge.

***Contrary*** : *adj.* 1. opposed, opposite, disagreeing, conflicting, opposing; 2. disagreeable, hostile, perverse, stubborn, headstrong; *Ant.* 1. similar, like, complementary. 2. obliging, agreeable, tractable.

***Contrast.*** : *n.* difference, distinction, disagreement; *vb.* distinguish, differentiate, contradict, differ; *Ant. n.* similarity, agreement, likeness.

***Contribute*** : *vb.* donate, give, bestow, grant, provide, offer; *Ant.* withhold, deny.

***Controversy*** : *n.* dispute, argument, quarrel, debate, disagreement; *Ant.* agreement, harmony, accord.

***Convenience*** : *n.* 1. availability, accessibility; 2. assistance, help, aid, service, benefit; *Ant.* 2. inconvenience.

***Convenient*** : *adj.* accessible, handy, nearby, available, ready; *Ant.* inconvenient, awkward.

***Conventional*** : *adj.* everyday, common, usual, regular, habitual, accustomed, routine; *Ant.* unusual, extraordinary, exotic, bizarre.

***Cool*** : *adj.* 1. chilly, cold, frosty, wintry, icy, frigid; 2. calm, composed, quiet, collected; 3. unfriendly, distant, chilly; *vb.* 1. chill; 2. calm, quiet, moderate; *Ant. adj.* 1. warm, hot, heated; 2. excited, over-wrought, hysterical; 3. friendly, warm, outgoing; *vb.* 1. warm, heat; 2. excite, agitate.

***Copious*** : *adj.* plentiful, abundant, ample; *Ant.* scarce, meagre, scanty, paltry.

***Copy*** : *n.* reproduction, imitation, facsimile, duplicate, likeness, carbon, print; *vb.* reproduce, duplicate, imitate; *Ant. n.* original.

***Cordial*** : *adj.* friendly, polite, genial, affable, warm-hearted; *Ant.* hostile, unfriendly, ill-tempered.

***Core*** : *n.* centre, kernel, heat; *Ant.* outside, surface.

***Correct*** : *adj.* true, accurate, right, proper, precise, exact; *vb.* 1. set right, rectify, amend, better; 2. warn, caution, rebuke, admonish, punish; *Ant. adj.* incorrect, wrong, inexact, erroneous.

***Correspond*** : *vb.* 1. match, compare, agree, coincide, fit, suit; 2. communicate, write; *Ant.* 1. diverge, differ, vary.

***Corrupt*** : *adj.* 1. dishonest, untrustworthy, crooked, treacherous, unscrupulous; 2. wicked, debased, low, evil, perverted; *vb.* bribe, demoralise, degrade; *Ant. adj.* 1. honest, upright, scrupulous; 2. pure, sanctified. *vb.* purify, edify, sanctify.

***Costly*** : *adj.* expensive, dear, high-priced; *Ant.* inexpensive, low-cost, cheap.

***Countenance*** : *n.* 1. face, visage, aspect, appearance; 2. approval, support, encouragement, assistance; *vb.* approve, support, favour, encourage; *Ant. vb.* prohibit, forbid.

***Counterfeit*** : *adj.* 1. fake, false, fraudulent, spurious, false; 2. pretended, pretend, false, fake, sham; *n.* forgery, imitation, fake; *vb.* 1. forge, fake, falsify, imitate, copy; 2. pretend, sham; *Ant. adj.* genuine, real, authentic.

***Courage*** : *n.* bravery, spirit, daring, fearlessness, valour, mettle, pluck; *Ant.* cowardice, fearfulness, weakness.

***Courageous*** : *adj.* brave, fearless, dauntless, intrepid, plucky, daring, heroic, valorous; *Ant.* cowardly, fearful, timid.

***Courteous*** : *adj.* polite, well-mannered, gracious, respectful *Ant.* rude, impolite, discourteous.

***Courtesy*** : *n.* politeness, graciousness, respect; *Ant.* rudeness, discourtesy.

***Cover*** : *vb.* 1. overlay, spread; 2. conceal, hide, mask; 3. include, embrace *n.* 1. lid, top, stopper, covering; 2. shelter, protection, refuge; *Ant. vb.* uncover, expose, reveal.

***Coward*** : *n.* milksop, milquetoast, dastard, cad; *Ant.* hero.

***Coy*** : *adj.* bashful, shy, timid, modest; *Ant.* bold, brash, forward.

***Craft*** : *adj.* cunning, clever, shrewd, skillful, sly, tricky; *Ant.* guileless, gullible, open, naive.

***Cranky*** : *adj.* bad-tempered, short-tempered, cross, testy, irritable; *Ant.* good-natured, cheerful, happy.

***Crave*** : *vb.* desire, yearn for, want, long for, hunger for; *Ant.* renounce, relinquish.

***Crazy*** : *adj.* mad, insane, lunatic; *Ant.* sane, rational, lucid.

***Create*** : *vb.* 1. originate, invent, beget; 2. make form, construct, design; *Ant.* destroy, abolish.

***Credible*** : *adj.* believable, conceivable; *Ant.* incredible, unbelievable, inconceivable.

***Credit*** : *n. 1.* belief, trust, faith; 2. honour, merit, recognition;

3. repute, reputation, name, standing, rank; *vb.* 1. belive, accept, trust; 2. attribute; *Ant. n.* discredit.

***Creditable*** : *adj.* praiseworthy, worthy; *Ant.* discreditable, dishonourable, shameful.

***Critical*** : *adj.* 1. faultfinding, carping, condemning, reproachful, dispproving; 2. dangerous, risky, hazardous, perilous; 3. crucial, important, decisive; *Ant.* 3. unimportant, trivial.

***Crooked*** : *adj.* 1. bent, twisted, curved, hooked, zigzag; 2. dishonest, criminal, corrupt; *Ant.* 1. straight, 2. honest, upright.

***Cross*** : *vb.* 1. traverse; 2. mingle, mix, interbreed; 3. thwart, frustrate, oppose; *Adj.* irritable, annoyed, testy, cranky, ill-natured, bad-tempered, snappish, mean, angry; *Ant. adj.* goodnatured cheerful.

***Crouch*** : *vb.* stoop, duck; *Ant.* stand.

***Crude*** : *adj.* 1. unfinished, rude, raw, coarse; 2. unpolished, unrefined, coarse, graceless, boorish; *Ant.* 1 finished, polished; 2. refined, genteel, cultured.

***Cruel*** : *adj.* heartless, mean, merciless, unmerciful, pitiless, ruthless, brutal, inhuman; *Ant.* kindhearted, compassionate, merciful.

***Cruelty*** : *n.* meanness, harshness, brutality, savagery; *Ant.* kindness, compassion.

***Cry*** : *vb.* 1. shout, yell, yowl, scream, roar, bellow; 2. weep, wail, sob, bawl; *Ant.* 2. laugh.

***Cunning*** : *adj.* 1. clever, tricky, wily, foxy, crafty; 2. skillful, clever, ingenious; *n.* 1. skill, ability; 2. craft, witness, foxiness, shrewdness, cleverness, slyness, deceit; *Ant. adj.* 1. simple, naive, gullible; *n.* 2. simplicity, openness.

***Curb*** : *n.* check, restraint, control *vb.* check, restrain, control. *Ant. vb.* encourage, foster.

***Curious*** : *adj.* 1. inquiring, inquisitive, interested, nosy, prying; 2. peculiar, odd, strange, unusual, queer; *Ant.* 1. incurious; indifferent, uninterested.

***Current*** : *adj.* present, up-to-date, modern; *Ant.* out-of-date, outmoded, old-fashioned.

***Curse*** : *n.* 1. oath, ban; 2. trouble, misfortune, evil; *vb.* swear, denounce, condemn; *Ant. n.* 1. benediction; 2. blessing, boon, advantage.

***Customary*** : *adj.* usual, common, habitual, regular; *Ant.* unusual, rare.

# D

***Dainty*** : *adj.* delicate, petite, pretty, beautiful, graceful, fine, elegant; *Ant.* clumsy, oafish, lumpish.

***Damage*** : *n.* impairment, injury, harm, destruction; *vb.* impair, injure, harm, mar; *Ant. vb.* repair, rebuild, improve, fix.

***Damp*** : *adj.* moist, dank, humid; *n.* moisture, dampness, dankness, humidity, wetness; *Ant. adj.* dry, arid.

***Danger*** : *n.* peril, risk, hazard, uncertainty, threat; *Ant.* safety, security.

***Dangerous*** : *adj.* perilous, hazardous, risky, uncertain, unsafe; *Ant.* safe, secure.

***Daring*** : *adj.* brave, fearless, intrepid, courageous, bold, valiant; *n.* bravery, courage, valour; *Ant. n.* cowardice, timidity.

***Dark*** : *adj.* 1. shadowy, unlit, murky, gloomy, dim, dusky, shaded, sunless, black; 2. dismal, sad, gloomy, unhappy; *Ant.* 1. light, illuminated, bright; 2. cheerful, happy.

***Daunt*** : *vb.* frighten, discourage, intimidate; *Ant.* encourage, enspirit.

***Dauntless*** : *adj.* brave, fearless, undaunted, bold, intrepid, courageous, valiant; *Ant.* cowardly, timid, fearful.

***Dawn.*** : *n.* 1. sunrise, daybreak 2. beginning, origin, start; *Ant.* 1. sunset, dusk, nightfall; 2. end, finish, conclusion.

***Dead*** : *adj.* 1. deceased, lifeless, defunct, gone, departed; 2. inert, motionless, still, inoperative, inoperable, inactive; *Ant.* 1. alive, animate; 2. active, functioning.

***Deaf*** : *adj.* 1. unhearing, stone-deaf; 2. unheeding, unheedful, unaware, stubborn, inattentive, oblivious; *Ant.* 2. conscious, aware.

***Dear*** : *adj.* 1. loved, beloved, darling; 2. expensive, costly, highpriced; *Ant.* 1. hateful; 2. cheap, inexpensive, reasonable.

***Death*** : *n.* demise, decease, passing, extinction; *Ant.* life.

***Decay*** : *vb.* 1. rot, spoil, decompose; 2. deteriorate, decline, wither, perish, die; *n.* 1. decline, downfall, collapse; 2. rot, decomposition, mold, rottenness; *Ant. vb.* grow, progress, flourish.

***Deceit*** : *n.* deceitfulness, deception, fraud, dishonesty, guile; *Ant.* honesty, forthrightness, openness.

***Deceitful*** : *adj.* insincere, false, dishonest, fraudulent, deceptive; *Ant.* honest, sincere.

***Decent*** : *adj.* proper, becoming, fitting, appropriate; *Ant.* indecent, improper, indecorous, unsuitable.

***Deception*** : *n.* trickery, treachery, craftiness, deceit; *Ant.* honesty, openness, frankness, probity.

***Deceptive*** : *adj.* deceiving, false, misleading, unreliable, tricky, deceitful, dishonest; *Ant.* real, true, authentic.

***Decide*** : *vb.* determine, settle, choose, resolve; *Ant.* hesitate, waver.

***Declare*** : *vb.* say, state, proclaim, announce, pronounce, affirm, assert; *Ant.* deny, suppress.

***Decline*** : *vb.* 1. refuse, deny, reject; 2. lessen, deteriorate, weaken, fail, diminish; *n.* 1. lessening, weakening, diminution; 2. decent, slope, incline, hill; *Ant. vb.* 1. agree, accept; 2. improve, increase, grow; *n.* 1. improvement.

***Decorate*** : *vb.* 1. ornament, paint, colour, enhance; 2. furnish, furbish; *Ant.* 1. deface, mar.

***Decrease*** : *vb.* lessen, diminish, decline, dwindle; *n.* lessening, diminution, decline; *Ant. vb.* increase, expand; *n.* increase, expansion.

***Deduct*** : *vb.* substract, eliminate, take away; *Ant.* add.

***Deep*** : *adj.* 1. low, bottomless, unplumbed; 2. serious, acute, bad, grave; 3. profound, obscure; 4. absorbed, involved; *n.* ocean, sea; *Ant. adj.* 1. shallow.

***Deface*** : *vb.* mar, scratch, disfigure, mutilate; *Ant.* beautify, decorate.

***Defeat*** : *vb.* 1. overcome, conquer, vanquish, overthrow, suppress; 2. thwart, foil, spoil, frustrate; *n.* conquest, overthrow; *Ant. vb.* 1. surrender, submit, yield.

***Defect*** : *n.* flaw, weakness, imperfection, blemish; *vb.* desert, abandon, leave, forsake; *Ant. n.* perfection, flawlessness. *vb.* join, support.

***Defective*** : *adj.* flawed, faulty, inoperable, inoperative, imperfect; *Ant.* perfect, flawless, faultless.

***Defend*** : *vb.* 1. protect, guard, safeguard, shield; 2. uphold, maintain; *Ant.* attack.

***Defer*** : *vb.* delay, put off, postpone; *Ant.* hurry, expedite, speed.

***Defiant*** : *adj.* antagonistic, obstinate, rebellious; *Ant.* submissive, yielding.

***Defile*** : *vb.* corrupt, pollute, debase; *Ant.* purify.

***Definite*** : *adj.* 1. certain, sure, positive, determined; 2. clear, sharp, distinct, obvious, plain; *Ant.* indefinite, undetermined.

***Defy*** : *vb.* challenge, oppose, dare, flout; *Ant.* yield, submit, surrender.

***Dejected*** : *adj.* depressed, unhappy, disheartened, discouraged, downhearted, sad; *Ant.* happy, cheerful, optimistic.

***Delay*** : *vb.* 1. postpone, put off, defer; 2. slow, hinder, retard; pause, hesitate; *n.* slowdown, postpone; *Ant. vb.* hasten, forward, advance.

***Delete*** : *vb.* cancel, erase, remove, cross out; *Ant.* add.

***Deliberate*** : *adj.* 1. purposeful, intentional, studied, considered, planned, calculated, premeditated; 2. slow, methodical, careful; *vb.* weigh, judge, consider, reflect; *Ant. adj.* 1. accidental, unintentional, unplanned.

***Delicate*** : *adj.* 1. dainty, fine, fragile, frail; 2. frail, weak, precarious; 3. sensitive, critical, demanding; *Ant.* 1. clumsy, heavy-handed, coarse; 2. hale, hearty, strong.

***Delicious*** : *adj.* savoury, delectable, appetising, luscious; *Ant.* unpleasant, unpalatable.

***Delight*** : *n.* pleasure, joy, enjoyment; *vb.* please, entertain, satisfy; *Ant. n.* revulsion, disgust, displeasure. *vb.* displease, revolt, disgust.

***Delightful*** : *adj.* charming, pleasing, refreshing, pleasant, pleasurable; *Ant.* disagreeable, unpleasant, nasty.

***Deliver*** : *vb.* 1. transport, carry, convey; 2. present, give, offer, address; 3. liberate, set free, release, save; *Ant.* 3. confine, imprison, enslave.

***Demand*** : *vb.* 1. request, call for ask, for, claim; 2. challenge, command, charge, direct; 3. require, need; *n.* 1. request, claim; 2. requirement, obligation; 3. market, interest, call; *Ant. vb.* 1. relinquish, waive.

***Demolish*** : *vb.* destroy, ruin, raze, devastate; *Ant.* build, construct, erect.

***Demolition*** : *n.* destruction, wrecking; *Ant.* construction, crection.

***Dense*** : *adj.* thick, solid, packed, compact, crowded; *Ant.* sparse, scanty.

***Deny*** : *vb.* 1. contradict, confute, repudiate, gainsay, dispute; 2. refuse, reject, disallow; *Ant.* 1. admit, concede, confess 2. allow, permit.

***Depart*** : *vb.* leave, go, withdraw; *Ant.* arrive, come.

***Deposit*** : *vb.* 1. put, place, put down; 2. save, bank, store; *n.* sediment, lees, dregs; 2. addition, entry; *Ant. vb.* withdraw; *n.* 2. withdrawal.

***Depress*** : *vb.* 1. dispirit, dishearten, discourage, dampen; 2. devalue, devaluate, cheapen; *Ant.* 1. cheer, exhilarate, exalt.

***Depression*** : *n.* 1. cavity, dip, hole, pothole, dent; 2. despair, gloom, melancholy, sorrow, sadness, hopelessness; 3. decline, recession, hard times; *Ant.* 1. elevation eminence; 2. elation, happiness; 3. boom.

***Deprive*** : *vb.* deny, strip; *Ant.* supply, provide, provision.

***Depth*** : *n.* deepness, profundity; *Ant.* height, tallness, loftiness.

***Descend*** : *vb.* move lower, climb down ; *Ant.* ascend, climb, mount.

***Desert*** : *vb.* abandon, leave, forsake, quit; *Ant.* join, accompany.

***Deserter*** : *n.* fugitive, runaway, defector, renegade; *Ant.* loyalist.

***Desirable*** : *adj.* wanted, sought-after, wished-for, coveted; *Ant.* unattractive, repellent.

***Desire*** : *vb.* 1. crave, long for, want, covet; 2. ask, request; *n.* need, longing, want, craving, wish; *Ant. vb.* 1. loathe, abhor, detest.

***Desolate*** : *adj.* 1. deserted, empty, lonely; 2. miserable, sad, unhappy, wretched; *Ant.* 1. crowded, populous, teeming;

2. cheerful, happy.

***Despair*** : *n.* hopelessness, desperation, discouragement; *vb.* lose heart, lose hope; *Ant. n.* joy, hope, optimism.

***Desperate*** : *adj.* despairing, hopeless, reckless; *Ant.* calm, collected.

***Despicable*** : *adj.* mean, base, contemptible, worthless; *Ant.* admirable, honourable, worthy.

***Despise*** : *vb.* scorn, dislike, disdain, condemn; *Ant.* admire, like, honour.

***Destroy*** : *vb.* 1. ruin, demolish, raze, waste; 2 kill, slay, end, extinguish; *Ant.* 1. create, start, undertake.

***Destruction*** : *n.* devastation, demolition, ruin, extinction; *Ant.* creation, beginning:

***Detain*** : *vb.* delay, restrain, hold back, stay, retard; *Ant.* forward, hurry, rush.

***Detest*** : *vb.* despise, hate, loathe *Ant.* like, love, appreciate, savour.

***Develop*** : *vb.* 1. grow expand, enlarge, advance, mature; 2. reveal, become known unfold; *Ant.* 1. deteriorate, degenerate.

***Devote*** : *vb.* apply, dedicate, give; with; *Ant.* relinquish, withdraw, withhold, ignore.

***Devout*** : *adj.* religious, pious, devoted; *Ant.* indifferent, scronful.

***Die*** : *vb.* 1. decease, perish, expire, go, pass away; 2. decrease, diminish, fade, sink, decline, wither, wane, fail; *Ant.* 2. flourish, grow.

***Difference*** : *n.* disagreement, inequality, contrast; *Ant.* similarlity, likeliness, kinship, compatibility.

***Different*** : *adj.* 1. unalike, unlike, differing, changed; 2. various, miscellaneous; *Ant.* 1. similar, alike, identical.

***Difficult*** : *adj.* 1. hard; 2. intricate, complicated. obscure; *Ant.* 1. easy; 2. simple.

***Difficulty*** : *n.* 1. hardship, trouble; 2. predicament, fix, trouble; *Ant.* 1. ease.

***Dignify*** : *vb.* elevate, honour; *Ant.* humiliate, degrade, shame.

***Dim*** : *adj.* unclear, faint, shadowy, vague; 1. *Ant.* bright, brilliant; *vb.* obscure, dull, darken; 2. *Ant.* brighten, illuminate.

***Diminish*** : *vb.* lesson, shrink, reduce, wane; *Ant.* enlarge, increase, wax.

***Diminutive*** : *adj.* little, small, tiny, wee, minute; *Ant.* big, large, great, huge, gigantic.

***Diplomatic*** : *adj.* polite, tactful, gracious, discreet, *Ant.* impolite, rude, thoughtless, ungracious.

***Direct*** : *vb.* 1. command, manage, control, regulate; 2. aim, sight, point, level; 3.indicate, guide, conduct, show; *adj.* 1. straight, unswerving; 2. plain, straightforward, frank, sincere, earnest; *Ant. adj.* 1. crooked, indirect, swerving. 2. dishonest, untruthful.

***Dirty*** : *adj.* solted, unclean, filthy, polluted; I *Ant.* clean, spotless, pure; *vb.* soil, foul, befoul, spot, pollute; *Ant.* clean, cleanse, purify.

***Disable*** : *vb.* cripple, incapacitate, weaken; *Ant.* strengthen.

***Disdvantage*** : *n.* 1. inconvenience, drawback; 2. handicap, hindrance, obstacle; benefit, advantage, convenience.

***Disappear*** : *vb.* vanish; end; *Ant.* appear, emerge.

***Di.appoint*** : *vb.* fail, dissatisfy; mislead; *Ant.* satisfy, please, gratify.

***Disappointment*** : *n.* defeat, dissatisfaction, failure, discouragement; *Ant.* satisfaction, pleasure, gratification.

***Discharge*** : *vb.* 1. relieve, unload, unburden; 2. fire, school; 3. let go, dismiss; *Ant.* 3. employ, hire, enlist. *n.* 1.

explosion, firing, detonation; 2. release, liberation; dismissal; 2. enlistment.

***Disciple*** : *n.* follower; supporter; student, pupil; *Ant.* leader, guide.

***Discipline*** : *n.* 1. training, practice, exercise, drill; 2. order. control, regulation; *vb.* 1. train, control, drill, teach; 2. punish, correct, chastise; *Ant.* *n.* 2. carelessness, negligence, sloppiness, messiness.

***Disclose*** : *vb.* reveal, show, expose, uncover; *Ant.* hide, disguise, mask, conceal.

***Disconnect*** : *vb.* separate, divide, unhook; detach, disengage; *Ant.* connect, engage, attach, bind, unify.

***Discontinue*** : *vb.* cease, end, stop, interrupt; *Ant.* begin, start, launch, initiate.

***Discord*** : *n.* conflict, disagreement; *Ant.* agreement, accord, concord.

***Discourge*** : *vb.* dispirit, dishearten, depress; *Ant.* encourage, inspire, inspirit.

***Discover*** : *vb.* find; learn, find out, ascertain, determine; *Ant.* conceal, hide.

***Discreet*** : *adj.* tactful, judicious, prudent, wise; cautious, careful; *Ant.* careless, incautious, tactless, indiscreet, imprudent.

***Disdain*** : *vb.* scron, reject, *Ant.* admire, respect, esteem, prize; *n.* scorn, contempt, haughtiness; *Ant.* admiration, respect, honour.

***Disdainful*** : *adj.* scornful, contemptuous, haughty, arrogant; *Ant.* admiring, awed regardful.

***Disgrace*** : *n.* shame, dishonour, embarrassment; *Ant.* honour, esteem; *vb.* shame, dishonour, embarrass, humiliate; *Ant.* honour, respect.

***Disguise*** : *vb.* mask, hide, screen, conceal, camoulflage;

*Ant.* reveal, dispalay, show.

***Disgust*** : *vb.* nauseate, sicken; offend, revolt, repulse; *n.* distaste, nausea, aversion, revulsion; *Ant. n.* likeing, admiration.

***Disgusting*** : *adj.* revolting, repulsive, nauseous, nauseating, repugnant; *Ant.* attractive, appealing.

***Dishonest*** : *adj.* corrupt, false, thievish; *Ant.* honest, straightforward, upright.

***Dismal*** : *adj.* gloomy, sorrowful, depressing, melancholy, dreary, sombre; *Ant.* cheerful, happy, charming, lighthearted.

***Dismay*** : *vb.* scare, frighten, alarm; discourage, dishearten; *Ant.* hearten, encourage.

***Dismiss*** : *vb.* discharge, release, let go, liberate; *Ant.* engage, employ, hire.

***Disorder*** : *n.* confusion, turmoil, tumult, chaos; *Ant.* order, neatness, organisation.

***Dispatch*** : *vb.* 1. send off or away 2. conclude, achieve, finish *n.* 1. message, report, communication, communique; 2. speed, promptness, quickness, swiftness; *Ant. n.* 2. slowness, reluctance, hestitancy.

***Disperse*** : *vb.* scatter, spread (out), separate; *Ant.* gather, collect, assemble.

***Display*** : *vb.* 1. exhibit, show, demonstrate; 2. reveal, uncover, show; *n.* showing, exhibit, exhibition, demonstration; *Ant. vb.* 2. disguise, hide, conceal, cover.

***Dispute*** : *vb.* argue, debate, quarrel, contest; 2. oppose, deny, contradict; *n.* argument, quarrel, debate, controversy; *Ant. vb.* agree, concur; *n.* agreement, accord, concurrence.

***Disrespectful*** : *adj.* rude, impudent, fresh, impolite, impertinent; cheeky; *Ant.* respectful, polite, courteous.

***Distant*** : *adj.* remote, far, afar, away, separated; *Ant.* near, close.

***Distinct*** : *adj.* 1. individual, separate, different; 2. clear, definite, obvious, plain; *Ant.* 2 indistinct, vague, uncertain, obscure.

***Distinguish*** : *vb.* 1. separate, divide, differentiate, classify; 2. perceive, discern, recognise; *Ant.* 1. blend, join, confuse.

***Distinguished*** : *adj.* renowned, famous, honoured, eminent, illustrious, noted, important, celebrated; *Ant.* obscure, unknown, undistinguished.

***Distract*** : *vb.* 1. divert, occupy; 2. confuse, bewilder; *Ant.* 2. concentrate, focus.

***Distress*** : *n.* 1. anguish, trouble, anxiety, worry, wretchedness; pain, 2. danger, peril; disaster; *vb.* worry, trouble, grieve, make wretched; *Ant. n.* 1. happiness, tranquillity, peacefulness; *vb.* please, charm, satisfy.

***Distribute*** : *vb.* share, deal, dispense, issue, dole, mete out; allocate, apportion; *Ant.* collect, gather, assemble.

***Distrust*** : *vb.* suspect, doubt, mistrust; *n.* suspicion, doubt, mistrust; *Ant. vb.* trust, *n.* trust, confidence.

***Disturb*** : *vb.* 1. annoy, bother, vex; 2. worry, trouble; *Ant.* calm, pacify.

***Disturbance*** : *n.* 1. commotion, disorder, confusion; 2. disorder, riot, brawl, fight; *Ant.* calm, serenity, tranquillity.

***Diverge*** : *vb.* branch off, separate, fork; *Ant.* join, converge, merge.

***Diversion*** : *n.* distraction, entertainment, amusement, sport, recreation; *Ant.* routine.

***Divert*** : *vb.* 1. turn aside or away, deflect; 2. amuse, entertain, distract; *Ant.* 2. bore, tire, weary.

***Divide*** : *vb.* 1. separate, split, part, detach, sever, cleave; 2. apportion, share, allot, allocate, distribute, deal *or* parcel *or* dole out; 3. disunite, split up, estrange; *Ant.* 1.

join, merge, combine 2. gather, collect; 3. unite, unify.

***Division*** : *n.* 1. separation, partition, sharing; 2. section, part, segment, portion; *Ant.* 1. agreement, union.

***Divulge*** : *vb.* reveal, release, disclose, expose; admit; *Ant.* conceal, hide.

***Dizzy*** : *adj.* giddy, unsteady, lightheaded; *Ant.* clearheaded, rational, unconfused.

***Domestic*** : *adj.* 1. home-loving 2. native, home-grown, homeade; *Ant.* 2. foreign, alien, outside.

***Doubt*** : *vb.* distrust, mistrust, question, suspect; *n.* 1. uncertainty, indecision, misgiving, skepticism, disbelief; 2. indecision, hesitancy; *Ant. vb.* trust, believe; *n.* belief, trust, confidence, reliance.

***Doubtful*** : *adj.* dubious, uncertain, questionable, unsettled, undermined, unsure; *Ant.* certain, definite, sure, settled.

***Downcast*** : *adj.* dejected, sad, depressed, downhearted, discouraged, unhappy, dispirited, despondent, crestfallen; *Ant.* cheerful, happy, lighthearted, encouraged.

***Downgrade*** : *vb.* lower, reduce, decrease, diminish, depreciate; *Ant.* upgrade, improve, appreciate.

***Downhearted*** : *adj.* sad, gloomy, depressed, downcast; *Ant.* cheerful, happy, enthusiastic.

***Drain*** : *vb.* 1. draw off, empty, tap; 2. exhaust, empty, sap, waste; milk; *n.* tap, duct, channel, pipe; *Ant. vb.* fill. fulfill.

***Dread*** : *vb.* fear; fear terror, horror; *Ant. n.* confidence, security.

***Dreary*** : *adj.* dismal, gloomy, cheerless, chilling, depressing; *Ant.* cheerful, hopeful, bright, encouraging.

***Dress*** : *n.* 1. gown, frock, costume; 2. attire, garb, wardrobe, clothing, garments, clothes, appearel, habit, livery; *vb.*

1. clothe, garb, don, wear, attire, robe; 2. prepare, treat, attend; *Ant. vb.* 1. undress, disrobe, strip.

***Droop*** : *vb.* sag, sink, settle; *Ant.* straighten, rise.

***Dry*** : *adj.* 1. arid, dehydrated, waterless, parched; 2. dull, boring, tedious, tiresome; *vb.* dehydrate, dessicate; *adj.* 1. wet, soaked, moist; 2. interesting, attractive, fascinating.

***Dull*** : *adj.* 1. boring, tiring, tiresome, uninteresting; 2. blunt, dulled; 3. slow, dumb, stupid, unimaginative; 4. unfeeling, insensible, lifeless, dead; *Ant.* 1. fascinating, interesting, engaging; 2. sharp, keen; 3. bright, intelligent, quick; 4 alert, animated, spirited.

***Dumb*** : *adj.* 1. dull, stupid ignorant; 2. speechless, mute; *Ant.* 1. intelligent, bright, lucid, quick.

***Dutiful*** : *adj.* faithful, obedient, docile; *Ant.* wilful, disobedient, headstrong, unruly.

***Dwarf*** : *n.* runt, midget; *vb.* stunt, reduce, minimise; *adj.* dwarfish tiny, minuscule; *Ant. n.* giant.

***Dwindle*** : *vb.* diminish, wane, lessen, decrease; *Ant.* increase, wax, gain, grow.

# E

***Eager*** : *adj.* keen, fervent, enthusiastic; ***Ant.*** indifferent, uninterested, univolved.

***Earnest*** : *adj.* sincere, serious, determined, eager; *Ant.* insincere, frivolous, indifferent.

***Earthly*** : *adj.* worldly, everyday, mundane; *Ant.* heavenly.

***Earthy*** : *adj.* 1. earthen, earthlike; 2. coarse, unrefined, crude, vulgar; *Ant.* 2. refined, elegant, tasteful.

***Ease*** : *n.* 1. comfort, rest, relaxation, repose, contentment, contentedness; 2. naturalness, facility, skillfulness, cleverness; *vb.* comfort, relieve, alleviate, soothe; lighten, lessen, reduce; *Ant. n.* 2. difficulty, trouble, effort; *vb.* aggravate, worsen, heighten, intensify.

***Easy*** : *adj.* 1. simple, effortless; 2. comfortable, unhurried, leisurely; *Ant.* difficult, awkward, strenuous.

***Economical*** : *adj.* thrify, provident, spring, careful, frugal; *Ant.* wasteful, lavish, unsparing.

***Ecstasy*** : *n.* rapture, delight, pleasure; *Ant.* misery, unhappiness, agony.

***Edge*** : *n.* border, rim, brink, threshold, boundry, margin; *vb.*

1. border, trim; 2. inch, move little by little, sidle; *Ant.* *n.* middle, centre.

***Edgy*** : *adj.* nervous, tense, irritable, touchy; *Ant.* tranquil, undisturbed, peaceful, bland.

***Effect*** : *n.* 1. result, outcome, consequence, end; 2. significance, importance, meaning; 3. accomplish, achieve; 4. cause make; bring about; *Ant. n.* 1. cause.

***Effective*** : *adj.* productive, efficient, practical; *Ant.* ineffective, wasteful, useless.

***Effcient*** : *adj.* 1. effective, useful, serviceable; 2. competent, apt, adept, able, capable, talented skilled, clever; *Ant.* 1. useless, unworkable; 2. inefficient, ineffective, clumsy, awkward.

***Elaborate*** : *adj.* ornate, ornamented, decorated, decorative, complicated, complex; *vb.* decorate, embellish; develop, detail; *Ant. adj.* simple, unadorned, stark. *vb.* simplify, streamline.

***Elastic*** : *adj.* flexible; resilient, pliable; *Ant.* rigid, inflexible, stiff.

***Elegant*** : *adj.* fine, refined, cultivated; tasteful, choice; *Ant.* crude, unpolished, coarse, tasteless.

***Elementary*** : *adj.* 1. basic, primary, fundamental; 2. simple, uncomplicated; *Ant.* 2. complex, complicated, involved, sophisticated.

***Elevate*** : *vb.* raise, lift; *Ant.* lower, drop.

***Elude*** : *vb.* evade, avoid, dodge; *Ant.* include, add.

***Embrace*** : *vb.* 1. hug, clasp; 2. include, contain, cover; *Ant.* 2. exclude, bar.

***Emerge*** : *vb.* come forth, appear; surface; *Ant.* recede, retreat, disappear.

***Eminent*** : *adj.* distinguished, famous, celebrated, renowned, important, prominent; *Ant.* unknown, undistinguished, ordinary, commonplace.

***Emotional*** : *adj.* 1. passionate, ardent, stirring; 2. hysterical, overwrought, zealous, enthusiastic, impetuous; *Ant.* calm, tranquil, placid.

***Emphatic*** : *adj.* definite, positive, energetic, forceful, strong; *Ant.* quiet, lax, unforceful.

***Employ*** : *vb.* 1. use, utilise, apply; 2. hire, engage, retain; *Ant. vb.* 1. waste, ignore, disregard.

***Employee*** : *n.* worker, labourer, wage-earner, servant; *Ant.* employer, boss.

***Employer*** : *n.* boss, proprietor, owner, management, manager, superviser, superintendent; *Ant.* worker, employee.

***Empty*** : *adj.* vacant, unoccupied, void, blank; *vb.* void, unload, evacuate; *Ant. adj.* full, filled; *vb.* fill.

***Enchant*** : *vb.* charm, fascinate, delight, bewitch; *Ant.* bore, tire.

***Enclose*** : *vb.* surround, encircle; *Ant.* exclude.

***Encourage*** : *vb.* inspirit, support, inspire; *Ant.* discourage, dissuade, deter.

***End*** : *n.* 1. extremity, tail-end, termination; 2. limit, termination, bound; 3. finish, conclusion, termination, close; 4. aim, purpose, object, intent; stop, finish, terminate, close, halt; *Ant. n.* beginning, start, opening, launch; *vb.* begin, start, launch, initiate.

***Endow*** : *vb.* give, bestow; *Ant.* divest.

***Endure*** : *vb.* 1. last, continue, persist; 2. suffer, bear, undergo, experience; *Ant.* 1. fail, perish, die.

***Enemy*** : *n.* foe, adversary, opponent, antagonist, rival; *Ant.* friend, colleague, cohort, ally.

***Energetic*** : *adj.* vigorous, active, forceful, potent; *Ant.* lazy, indolent, sluggish, lax.

***Energy*** : *n.* power, force, strength, vigour; *Ant.* lethargy, feebleness.

***Engage*** : *vb.* 1. employ, occupy; 2. employ, hire, retain; *Ant.* 1. disengage; 2. fire, dismiss, discharge.

***Engaging*** : *adj.* beguiling, enchanting, charming; *Ant.* boring, ordinary.

***Enjoyment*** : *n.* delight, pleasure, gratification; *Ant.* displeasure, abhorrence.

***Enlarge*** : *vb.* increase, amplify, extend, expand; magnify *Ant.* decrease, diminish, wane, shrink.

***Enlighten*** : *vb.* inform, teach, educate; *Ant.* confuse.

***Enlist*** : *vb.* enroll, enter, sign up, register; *Ant.* leave, abandon, quit.

***Enormous*** : *adj.* huge, immense, gigantic, vast, colossal, stupendous, gargantuan; *Ant.* small, diminutive, tiny, slight, infinitesimal.

***Enrage*** : *vb.* infuriate, anger, madden, *Ant.* soothe, appease, calm.

***Enroll*** : *vb.* enlist, register, sign up; *Ant.* leave, quit, abandon.

***Enterprising*** : *adj.* resourceful, energetic; *Ant.* indolent, lazy, unresourceful, sluggish.

***Entertain*** : *vb.* amuse, divert, interest; *Ant.* bore, tire.

***Enthusiasm*** : *n.* eagerness, zeal, earnestness; *Ant.* indifference, unconcern.

***Enthusiastic*** : *adj.* eager, zealous, earnest; *Ant.* indifferent, aloof, unconcerned.

***Entire*** : *adj.* whole, complete, intact, undivided; *Ant.* partial, incomplete, separated, divided.

***Entrance*** : *n.* entry, door, access, gate, opening; *Ant.* exit.

***Envy*** : *n.* jealousy, covetousness; *vb.* covet; *Ant. n.* generosity.

***Equal*** : *adj.* 1. equivalent; same, identical; 2. even, regular, uniform; *vb.* match; *Ant. adj.* 1. unequal, different; 2. uneven, irregular.

***Erase*** : *vb.* remove, obliterate, expunge, cancel; *Ant.* include. add.

***Erect*** : *adj.* upright, vertical, straight; *vb.* build, construct, raise; set up; *Ant. adj.* horizontal, flat; *vb.* demolish, raze, flatten.

***Erroneous*** : *adj.* mistaken, wrong, inaccurate, incorrect, false, untrue; *Ant.* correct, right, accurate, true.

***Essential*** : *adj.* important, necessary, vital, critical indispensable; *n.* necessity, requirement; *Ant. adj.* unimportant, dispensable, inessential, unnecessary.

***Establish*** : *vb.* found, form set up, begin; *Ant.* discontinue, disperse, scatter.

***Esteem*** : *vb.* prize, value, regard highly, revere, respect; *n.* respect, reverence, regard, honour, admiration; *Ant. vb.* disdain, disregard, scorn; *n.* scorn, contempt.

***Eternal*** : *adj.* everlasting, endless, perpetual; *Ant.* brief, passing, temporary, transient.

***Evade*** : *vb.* elude, escape, dodge; *Ant.* meet, confront, face.

***Evaporate*** : *vb.* vaporise; disappear, vanish; *Ant.* appear, condense.

***Even*** : *adj.* 1. level, smooth, flat; 2. equal, balanced, square; 3 parallel; *adv.*just, exactly; *Ant. adj.* 1. bumpy, irregular. 2. unequal, unbalanced; 3. divergent.

***Evening*** : *n.* dusk, twilight, nightfall, sundown; *Ant.* dawn, sunrise.

***Eventual*** : *adj.* ultimate, consequent; *Ant.* current, present.

***Ever*** : *adv.* 1. always, continuously, constantly; 2. at all, at any time; *Ant.* never.

***Evident*** : *adj.* clear, plain, obvious, apparent; *Ant.* unclear, obscure, doubtful, uncertain.

***Evil*** : *adj.* sinful, immoral, wicked, bad; 2. harmful injurious; *n.* harm, woe; badness, wickedness, sin; *Ant.adj.* 1. virtuous, moral, upright, good; 2. benefical, advantageous, useful; *n.* goodness, virtue, uprightness.

***Exact*** : *adj.* correct, accurate, errorless, faultless; *Ant.* inexact, inaccurate, faulty.

***Exaggerate*** : *vb.* overstate, magnify; *Ant.* minimise, understate, diminish.

***Excellence*** : *n.* superiority, distinction; *Ant.* inferiority, poorness, badness.

***Excellent*** : *adj.* fine, superior, wonderful, marvelous; *Ant.* inferior, poor, bad, terrible, sub standard.

***Exceptional*** : *adj.* unusual, different, strange, irregular, abnormal; *Ant.* unexceptional, ordinary, commonplace.

***Excess*** : *adj.* profuse, abundant, immoderate; *n.* profusion, lavishness; *Ant. adj.* sparse, inconsequential, meagre.

***Excite*** : *vb.* stir up, arouse, stimulate; move; *Ant.* lull, bore.

***Exclude*** : *vb.* keep out, shut out, bar, except; *Ant.* include, embrace, involve.

***Exclusion*** : *n.* bar, exception, rejection; *Ant.* inclusion.

***Exclusive*** : *adj.* 1. limited, restricted, restrictive, selective, 2. select, fashionable, choice; *Ant.* 1. general, unrestricted. 2. ordinary, unfashionable, common.

***Excuse*** : *vb.* forgive, pardon; *n.* explantion, reason, plea, apology; *Ant. vb.* condemn.

***Exhaust*** : *vb.* 1. tire, fatigue, wear out; 2. use, use up, consume; spend; *Ant.* 1. refresh, renew; 2. replenish, replace.

***Exhibit*** : *vb.* 1. show, display, demonstrate; 2. show, display, betray, reveal; *n.* show, display, demonstration, exhibition; *Ant. vb.* conceal, hide, disguise.

***Expand*** : *vb.* enlarge, swell, inflate; bloat; *Ant.* shrink, shrivel, contract.

***Expel*** : *vb.* drive out *or* away, discharge; banish, deport, exile; *Ant.* invite, accept.

***Expend*** : *vb.* use, consume, exhaust; *Ant.* conserve, reserve, ration.

***Expensive*** : *adj.* dear, costly, high-priced; *Ant.* inexpensive, modest, low-priced, low-cost, cheap.

***Experience*** : *n.* 1. encountering, living, existence; 2. knowledge, background, skill; *vb.* feel, live through; *Ant. n.* inexperience, naivete.

***Experienced*** : *adj.* skilled, accomplished, expert, practised, able, qualified; *Ant.* inexperienced, untutored, naive, unpractised.

***Expert*** : *n.* authority, specialist; *adj.* skillful, experienced, knowledgeable, skilled; *Ant. adj.* unskilled, untrained, inexperienced.

***Expose*** : *vb.* reveal, bare, uncover, display, disclose; *Ant.* conceal, hide, cover, mask.

***Express*** : *vb.* state, declare; *adj.* 1. specific, precise, exact, special; 2. nonstop, quick, direct rapid fast; *Ant. adj.* 2. local.

***Extend*** : *vb.* 1. stretch, stretch out; 2. lengthen; 3. give, offer, grant; yield; *Ant.* 2. shorten, abbreviate, curtail.

***Extensive*** : *adj.* wide, broad, spacious, vast; *Ant.* confined, restricted, narrow.

***Exterior*** : *n.* outside, face, surface, covering *adj.* outside, outer, external; *Ant. n.* interior, inside, lining; *adj.* inner, internal, interior.

***External*** : *adj.* exterior, outer, outside; *Ant.* internal, interior, inner, inside.

***Extinct*** : *adj.* dead, lost, gone, vanished; *Ant.* alive, present, extant, flourishing.

***Extract*** : *vb.* draw out, withdraw, pull out, remove; *n.* essence, distillate; *Ant. vb.* insert, introduce, penetrate.

***Extraordinary*** : *adj.* unusual, exceptional, rare, uncommon, remarkable; *Ant.* ordinary, commonplace, usual.

***Extravagant*** : *adj.* wasteful, favish, excessive; *Ant.* frugal, economical, prudent, thrifty, provident.

***Extreme*** : *adj.* 1. utmost, greatest; 2. furthest, outermost, endmost, ultimate 3. excessive, immoderate; *n.* end, limit extremity; *Ant. adj.* 3. modest, moderate, reasonable.

# F

***Fabricate*** : *vb.* make, manufacture, assemble, construct, forms; *Ant.* destroy, demolish, raze.

***Fabulous*** : *adj.* fantastic, unbelievable, amazing, astonishing, astounding; *Ant.* commonplace, ordinary.

***Facility*** : *n.* 1. ease, skill, skillfulness, ability; 2. equipment, material; *Ant.* 1. difficulty, effort, labour.

***Factual*** : *adj.* correct, accurate, true; *Ant.* erroneous, invented, fabricated, incorrect.

***Fade*** : *vb.* 1. pale, bleach, discolour; 2. diminish, weaken, fail; *Ant.*2. increase, grow, wax.

***Fail*** : *vb.* 1. fall short, miss, founder; 2. dissappoint; 3. fade, weaken dwindle; *Ant.* 1. succeed.

***Failure*** : *n.* 1. failing, unsuccesfulness; 2. deficiency, insufficiency; *Ant.* success, achievement, accomplishment.

***Faint*** : *adj.* 1. dim, faded, indistinct; 2. feeble weak, half-hearted; *vb.* swoon, lose consciousness, collapse; *Ant.* *adj.* 1. clear, sharp, distinct; 2. strong, forceful, loud.

***Fainthearted*** : *adj.* timid, shy, bashful; cowardly; *Ant.* brave, courageous, stouthearted, fearless.

***Fair*** : *adj.* 1. just, impartial, unbiased, objective, unprejudiced; honest: 2. ordinary, average, not bad; 3. light, white, milky, blond; 4. beautiful; 5. sunny, pleasant, bright, unclouded; *Ant.* 1. unfair, unjust, blased; 3. dark. dusky, swarthy; 4. stormy, cloudy, threatening.

***Faith*** : *n.* 1. trust, reliance, belief; 2. belief, religion, creed; *Ant.* 1. mistrust, distrust, disbelief.

***Faithful*** : *adj.* 1. loyal, devoted, trustworthy, trusty, true; 2. credible accurate, strict; *Ant.* 1. disloyal, faithless, treacherous; 2. inaccurate, erroneous, wrong.

***Fake*** : *adj.* false, pretended, phony; *n.* fraud, cheat; counterfeit, forgery, imitation; *Ant. adj.* genuine, real, authentic.

***Fall*** : *vb.* 1. drop, descend, plunge; topple; 2. die; 3. lower, decrease, diminish; *n.* 1. autumn; 2. drop, decline, collapse, spill; *Ant. vb.* 1. rise, soar, ascend; 3. rise, increase, climb; *n.* 2. rise, ascent, increase.

***Falsehood*** : *n.* fib, story; untruth, lie; *Ant.* truth,

***Fame*** : *n.* name, reputation, renown, honour, glory; *Ant.* anonymity.

***Famed*** : *adj.* renowned, known, famous; *Ant.* unknown, anonymous, obscure.

***Familiar*** : *adj.* 1. known, common, frequent, well-known; 2. well-acquainted, friendly, close, intimate; 3. well-acquainted, well-versed; *Ant.* 1. unfamiliar, unknown, foreign, alien. 2. rare, distant; 3. ignorant, unaware.

***Familiarity*** : *n.* knowledge, understanding, awareness, comprehension; *Ant.* ignorance.

***Famine*** : *n.* want, hunger, starvation; *Ant.* plenty.

***Famous*** : *adj.* well-known, renowned, celebrated, famed, eminent, illustrious; *Ant.* unknown, obscure, anonymous.

***Fancy*** : *n.* imagination, fantasy; taste; *adj.* 1. ornate, ornamented, elaborate; 2. special, deluxe; *Ant. adj.* plain, unadorned, simple, undecorated.

***Fascinate*** : *vb.* attract, charm, bewitch, enchant; *Ant.* bore.

***Fashionable*** : *adj.* stylish, chic, modish, smart; *Ant.* unfashionable, dowdy.

***Fast*** : *adj.* 1. qucik, rapid, swift, speedy; 2. secure, solid, staunch, firm; *adv.* 1. quickly, rapidly, swiftly, speedily; 2. tightly, securely, firmly; *Ant. adj.* 1. slow, sluggish. 2. loose, insecure.

***Fasten*** : *vb.* attach, fix, join, secure, pin; *Ant.* loosen. loose, free, release, unclasp.

***Fat*** : *adj.* 1. fatty, oily, greasy; 2. obese, plump, fleshy, stout, chubby; 3. thick, wide; *Ant.* 2. thin, lean, emaciated, slim, scrawny.

***Fatigue*** : *n.* weariness, exhaustion, tiredness; *Ant.* energy.

***Faulty*** : *adj.* defective, imperfect, damaged, broken; *Ant.* perfect, flawless, whole.

***Favour*** : *n.* approval, liking, benefit; *vb.* 1. approve, like, prefer; 2. prefer, patronise, support; *Ant. vb.* disapprove, deplore.

***Fearless*** : *adj.* brave, courageous, bold; *Ant.* fearful, timid, cowardly.

***Feeble*** : *adj.* weak; frail, sickly, infirm; *Ant.* strong, powerful, potent.

***Ferocious*** : *adj.* fierce, savage, bloodthirsty, wild; *Ant.* gentle, playful, calm, harmless.

***Fertile*** : *adj.* productive, rich, fruitful; *Ant.* barren, sterile, unproductive.

***Festive*** : *adj.* merry, gay, joyful, joyous; *Ant.* sad, mournful, morose, gloomy.

***Fierce*** : *adj.* savage, ferocious, furious, violent, wild; *Ant.* gentle, peaceful, harmless.

***Filthy*** : *adj.* dirty, foul; polluted, contaminated; *Ant.* clean, pure, unspoiled.

***Final*** : *adj.* last, ultimate, terminal, concluding; *Ant.* first, initial, beginning, starting.

***Fine*** : *adj.* 1. excellent, superior, superb, choice, exquisite, perfect; 2. thin, minute; powdered; *Ant.* 1. inferior, poor, squalid; 2. coarse, broad.

***Finish*** : *vb.* 1. end, terminate, close, conclude; 2. consume, use up, complete; *n.* 1. conclusion, end, close, termination; 2. surface, patina, polish; *Ant. vb.* 1. begin, start, open; *n.* 1. opening, start, beginning.

***Firm*** : *adj.* 1. rigid, stiff, solid, unchanging, inflexible, steadfast, unshakable; 2. compact, dense, hard; *n.* company, business, concern; partnership, corporation; *Ant. adj.* 1. limp, drooping, soft, weak; '2. soft, squashy.

***Fitting*** : *adj.* suitable, apt, proper, due; *Ant.* unsuitable, inappropriate, improper.

***Flat*** : *adj.* 1. level, even, smooth; 2. dull, uninteresting, boring, lifeless; evenly, smoothly; *Ant. adj.* 1. uneven, rough, bumpy; 2. interesting, stimulating.

***Fleet*** : *adj.* swift, fast, rapid, quick; *Ant.* slow, sluggish.

***Fleeting*** : *adj.* temporary, brief, passing, swift; permanent, fixed, stable, lasting.

***Flexible*** : *adj.* 1. elastic, supple, pliant, pliable; 2. yielding, easy, agreeable, adaptable; *Ant:* inflexible, rigid, firm, unyielding, fixed.

***Flimsy*** : *adj.* weak, wobbly, frail, fragile; *Ant.* strong, firm, stable.

***Flourish*** : *vb.* 1. grow, succeed, prosper; 2. wave, brandish; *Ant.* 1. decline, die.

***Foe*** : *n.* enemy, adversary, antagonist, opponent; *Ant.* friend, ally.

***Follow*** : *vb.* 1. succeed, ensue; 2. obey, heed, observe; 3. chase, pursue, track; trace; *Ant.* 1. lead.

***Follower*** : *n.* pupil, disciple; *Ant.* leader.

***Fondness*** : *n.* liking, affection, partiality; *Ant.* unfriendliness, hostility.

***Foolish*** : *adj.* silly, senseless, stupid, simple; *Ant.* sensible, sound, reasonable, rational.

***Forbid*** : *vb.* ban, disallow, prohibit, prevent; *Ant.* allow, permit, let.

***Foreign*** : *adj.* strange, unfamiliar, alien, different, exotic; *Ant.* familiar, ordinary, commonplace.

***Foreigner*** : *n.* alien, stranger, outsider, newcomer; *Ant.* native, resident.

***Forever*** : *adv.* always, hereafter, evermore, everlastingly; *Ant.* temporarily, fleetingly.

***Forgive***: *vb.* pardon, excuse; *Ant.* censure, blame.

***Formal*** : *adj.* 1. conventional, conformist; 2. ceremonial, ritual; *Ant.* informal, unceremonious.

***Former*** : *adj.* previous, earlier, erstwhile, one-time; *Ant.* present, current.

***Forthright*** : *adj.* direct, honest, candid, frank, outspoken; *Ant.* devious, tricky, roundabout.

***Fortunate*** : *adj.* lucky, blessed, charmed; *Ant.* unfortunate, unlucky, cursed.

***Forward*** : *adv.* onward, ahead; 1. front, first, leading, foremost; 2. rude, bold, arrogant, fresh, impertinent, impudent; *Ant.* *adv.* backward, rearward; *adj.* 1. rearmost, last; 2. shy, demure, retiring.

***Foul*** : *adj.* 1. dirty, filthy, unclean, impure, polluted; 2. evil, wicked, vile, sinful; 3. stormy, bad, rainy; 1. clean, pure, immaculate; 2. saintly, good; 3. clear, sunny, calm.

***Fragile*** : *adj.* delicate, breakable, frail, weak; *Ant.* sturdy, hardy, stout, strong.

***Fragment*** : *n.* bit, part, piece, scrap, remnant; *Ant.* whole.

***Fragrant*** : *adj.* sweet-smelling, aromatic, perfumed, scented; *Ant.* malodorous, noxious, smelly.

***Frail*** : *adj.* weak, fragile, breakable, feeble, delicate; *Ant.* strong, sturdy, hardy, powerful.

***Frank*** : *adj.* candid, open, forthright, honest, unreserved, sincere, direct; *Ant.* devious, dishonest, tricky.

***Frantic*** : *adj.* wild, frenzied, delirious, excited, hysterical, mad, crazy; *Ant.* calm, tranquil, composed.

***Free*** : *adj.* 1. independent, unrestrained, unrestricted, liberated; 2. gratuitous, without charge; 3. loose, unfastened, unattached; *vb.* release, liberate, set free, emancipate; *Ant. vb.* enslave, entrap, snare.

***Freedom*** : *n.* liberty, independence; *Ant.* slavery, servitude, bondage.

***Frequent*** : *adj.* common, customary, habitual; *vb.* habituate, visit often; *Ant. adj.* infrequent, uncommon.

***Fresh*** : *adj.* 1. recent, new, current, late; 2. pure, sweet, drinkable, safe; 3. rested, healthy, energetic, vigorous; 4. different, original; 5. inexperienced, unskilled, untrained; *Ant.* 1. old, out-of-date; 2. impure, polluted; foul; 3. exhausted, tired. 4. state, unoriginal; 5. mature, seasoned, experienced.

***Fretful*** : *adj.* irritable, peevish, testy, touchy, short-tempered; *Ant.* calm, easygoing.

***Friend*** : *n.* companion, acquaintance, crony, chum, mate; *Ant.* enemy, foe.

***Front*** : *n.* 1. face, facade; 2. beginning, start, head; *vb.* face, border, look out on; *Ant. n.* 1., 2. back, rear.

***Frugal*** : *adj.* thrifty, economical, provident; *Ant.* improvident, spendthrift, prodigal.

***Fruitful*** : *adj.* fertile, productive, rich, abundant; *Ant.* barren, lean, unproductive, fruitless.

***Fruitless*** : *adj.* sterile, unproductive, barren; vain, futile; *Ant.* fruitful, productive, fertile.

***Frustrate*** : *vb.* defeat, discourage, prevent; *Ant.* satisfy.

***Full*** : *adj.* 1. filled, complete, replete; 2. taken, occupied, in use; *Ant.* empty, vacant.

***Funny*** : *adj.* humorous, amusing, droll, comic, comical, laughable; *Ant.* unamusing, unfunny, humourless.

***Furious*** : *adj.* enraged, angry; *Ant.* calm, serene.

***Fury*** : *n.* 1. rage, anger, wrath, frenzy; 2. violence, ferocity, ferociousness, fierceness; *Ant.* serenity, calmness.

***Futile*** : *adj.* 1. useless, pointless, vain, idle, worthless; 2. unimportant; minor, trivial; *Ant.* 1. worthwhile, valuable; 2. important, serious, weighty.

***Future*** : *adj.* coming, to come, approaching, impending, imminent, destined; *Ant.* past, bygone, former.

# G

***Gain*** : *vb.* 1. obtain, get, acquire, win, earn; 2. improve, better, advance; 3. increase in; *n.* 1. profit; 2. increase, improvement, advantage; *Ant. vb.* lose; *n.* loss.

***Gather*** : *vb.* 1. assemble, collect, accumulate, come or bring together; 2. understand, learn, assume; *Ant.* 1. disperse, scatter, dispel.

***Gay*** : *adj.* 1. joyful, joyous, jovial, gleeful, merry, cheerful, happy; 2. bright, colourful, brilliant; *Ant.* sad, mournful, somber, sorrowful.

***General*** : *adj.* 1. indefinite, miscellaneous, inexact, vague; 2. common, usual, regular, customary; *Ant.* 1. definite, specific, exact, precise.

***Generous*** : *adj.* 1. charitable, liberal, unselfish; 2. noble, big, honourable; *Ant.* 1. stingy, mean, selfish, tightfisted.

***Gentle*** : *adj.* 1. friendly, amiable, mild, kind; 2. fame, cultivated, civilised; *Ant.* 1. mean, nasty. 2. rough, uncouth.

***Genuine*** : *adj.* 1. real, actual, true; 2. sincere, unaffected, definite; *Ant.* 1. fake, bogus, counterfeit, false; 2. insincere, pretended, sham.

***Giant*** : *n.* colossus, Goliath, Cyclops, monster; *adj.* gigantic, huge, colossal, monstrous, enormous; *Ant. n.* dwarf, midget, runt; *adj.* small, tiny, minuscule, infinitesimal.

***Gigantic*** : *adj.* huge, enormous, giant, large; *Ant.* small, little, tiny, infinitesimal.

***Gingerly*** : *adj.* cautiously, gentle; *adv.* carefully, cautiously, gently; *Ant. adv.* roughly.

***Give*** : *vb.* 1. furnish, provide, donate, supply, contribute, grant, present; 2. yield, give in, give way; 3. produce, develop, yield; 4. sacrifice, give up, donate; *Ant. vb.* 1. take.

***Glad*** : *adj.* 1. pleased, happy, satisfied, delighted; 2. cheerful, happy, joyous, joyful; *Ant.* 1. unhappy, sad, morose; 2. gloomy, sombre, dismal.

***Gloom*** : *n.* 1. darkness, shade, shadows, dimness; 2. sadness, melancholy; *Ant.* 1. brightness. 2. cheerfulness, happiness.

***Gloomy*** : *adj.* 1. sad, melancholy, morose, downcast, downhearted, glum, unhappy; 2. dark, dim, shadowy, dismal; *Ant.* 1. happy, cheerful, merry, highspirited. 2. sunny, bright, shine.

***Go*** : *vb.* 1. leave, depart, withdraw; 2. proceed, move, travel; progress: 3. become; 4. agree, harmonise, fit, suit; 5. operate, function, work, run; 6. pass, elapse; *Ant. vb.* 1. come.

***Good*** : *adj.* 1. qualified, suited, suitable, apt, proper, capable, fit; 2. generous, kindly, kind, friendly, gracious, obliging; 3. pleasant, agreeable, pleasurable, satisfactory, fine; 4. well-behaved, obedient, proper; 5. healthy, sound, normal; 6. honourable, reliable, trustworthy, safe; 7. favourable, excellent, profitable; *n.* 1. benefit, welfare, advantage, profit; 2. virtue, righteousness; *Ant.* bad; 3. kindness, beneficence; *Ant.* evil.

***Goodness*** : *n.* honesty, virtue, good, integrity; *Ant.* dishonesty, badness, evil, corruption, sin.

***Gorgeous*** : *adj.* splendid, magnificent, grand, dazzling; *Ant.* ugly, homely, squalid.

***Gracious*** : *adj.* 1. kind, friendly; courteous, polite; 2. tender, merciful, mild, gentle; *Ant.* 1. rude,impolite, discourteous, thoughtless.

***Gradual*** : *adj.* little by little, slow, moderate; *Ant.* sudden, swift, abrupt.

***Grand*** : *adj.* 1. splendid, elaborate, great, royal, stately; 2. fine, noble dignified; 3. chief, principal, main; *Ant.* 1. humble, modest, unassuming.

***Grant*** : *vb.* 1. give, bestow, confer, award; 2. agree, allow, concede, accept; *n.* award, bequest, gift; *Ant. vb.* 1. deny.

***Grateful*** : *adj.* appreciative, thankful; *Ant.* ungrateful, thankless, grudging.

***Gravity***: *vb.* satisfy, please; *Ant.* frustrate.

***Grave*** : *adj.* 1. sober, thoughtful, solemn, serious; 2. important, serious, weighty; *Ant.* 1. happy, merry, frivolous, jolly. 2. trivial, unimportant.

***Gravity*** : *n.* seriousness, importance; concern; *Ant.* triviality.

***Great*** : *adj.* 1. large, big, huge, enormous, immense, gigantic; 2. noteworthy, worthy, distinguished, remarkable; 3. chief, leading, main, principal; *Ant.* 1. small, diminutive 2. insignificant, trivial; 3. minor.

***Greed*** : *n.* avarice, greediness, covetousness; *Ant.* generosity, selflessness, unselfishness.

***Greedy*** : *adj.* selfish, covetous, grasping, avaricious; *Ant.* generous, giving, unselfish.

***Grief*** : *n.* sorrow, sadness, distress, suffering, anguish, woe, misery; *Ant.* joy.

***Grieve*** : *vb.* 1. lament, mourn, weep; 2. distress, sorrow, sadden, hurt; *Ant.* rejoice, celebrate.

***Gross*** : *adj.* 1. improper, rude, coarse, indecent, crude, vulgar; 2. outrageous, extreme, grievous, shameful; *Ant.* 1. refined, cultivated, polite.

***Grow*** : *vb.* 1. enlarge, increase, swell, expand; 2. develop, flower; 3. cultivate, raise, produce, nurture; *Ant.* 1. shrink, decrease.

***Guard*** : *vb.* protect, preserve, shield, defend, protector, sentry, watchman, sentinel; *Ant. vb.* neglect, ignore, disregard.

***Guess*** : *vb.* suppose, think, imagine, believe; *n.* notion, opinion, hypothesis, theory; *Ant. vb.* know.

***Guest*** : *n.* visitor, caller, company; *Ant.* host.

***Guide*** : *vb.* 1. lead, direct, conduct, steer, pilot; 2. influence, affect; *n.* director, pilot, steersman, leader; *Ant. vb.* follow; *n.* follower.

***Guilty*** : *adj.* responsible, culpable, blameworthy; *Ant.* innocent, blameless, guiltless.

# H

***Haggard*** : *adj.* gaunt, drawn, worn, careworn; *Ant.* fresh, animated, bright, clear-eyed.

***Hale*** : *adj.* hearty, healthy, robust, vigorous; *Ant.* feeble, weak.

***Halfhearted*** : *adj.* indifferent, uncaring, cool, unenthusiastic; *Ant.* enthusiastic, eager, earnest.

***Halt*** : *vb.* stop, cease, hold; *n.* stop, end; *Ant. vb.* start, begin; *n.* start, beginning.

***Handily*** : *adv.* easily, readily, smoothly; *Ant.* awkwardly, clumsily, ineptly.

***Handsome*** : *adj.* 1. good-looking, fine, comely; 2. generous, large, big, liberal, ample; *Ant.* 1. ugly, homely, unattractive. 2. mean, petty, stingy, niggardly.

***Handy*** : *adj.* 1. ready, at hand, near, nearby, close; 2. helpful, clever, useful; *Ant.* inconvenient.

***Happiness*** : *n.* joy, delight, joyfulness, joyousness, elation, ecstasy; *Ant.* sadness, gloom, melancholy.

***Happy*** : *adj.* 1. pleased, contented, satisfied; 2. lucky, fortunate; *Ant.* 1. sad, gloomy, sorrowful; 2. unlucky, inconvenient, unfortunate.

***Hard*** : *adj.* 1. firm, solid, rigid, unyielding, compact, dense; 2. difficult, laborious, exhausting; 3. difficult, complicated, puzzling, tough, intricate; 4. severe, stern, harsh, strict, demanding; 5. shrewd, hardheaded, unsympathetic, cool, cold; *Ant. adj.* 1. soft, pliable, yielding; 2. easy, undemanding, comfortable; 3. simple, uncomplicated, direct; 4. lenient, easygoing.

***Harden*** : *vb.* solidify, petrify; *Ant.* soften, loosen.

***Hardy*** : *adj.* vigorous, sturdy, tough, strong; *Ant.* weak, feeble, frail, fragile, decrepit.

***Harmful*** : *adj.* mischievous, hurtful, injurious; *Ant.* beneficial, advantageous.

***Harmless*** : *adj.* innocent, painless; *Ant.* harmful, injurious, dangerous.

***Harmonious*** : *adj.* 1. melodious, tuneful; 2. amicable, congenial; *Ant.* 1. discordant, dissonant; 2. quarrelsome, discordant, disagreeable.

***Harmony*** : *n.* agreement, accord, unity; *Ant.* discordance, disagreement, conflict.

***Harsh*** : *adj.* 1. rough, severe, tough, unpleasant, unkind, stern, cruel; 2. rough, coarse, jarring; *Ant.* 1. easy, soothing, gentle. 2. melodious, pleasing.

***Haste*** : *n.* 1. rush, hurry, rapidity, speed; 2. scramble, hurry, flurry, rush; heedlessness; *Ant.* 1. sluggishness, sloth.

***Hasten*** : *vb.* 1. hurry, rush, run, scurry, scamper, dash, sprint; 2. hurry, rush, dispatch, quicken, urge, press, speed; *Ant.* 1. dawdle, linger, tarry.

***Hate*** : *vb.* detest, abhor, loathe, despise, disfavour, dislike; *n.* hatred, loathing, abhorrence; dislike; *Ant. vb.* like, love, admire. *n.* liking, love, esteem.

***Hateful*** : *adj.* detestable, loathsome, offensive; *Ant.* lovable, likable, admirable.

***Hatred*** : *n.* hate, loathing, aversion; *Ant.* liking, appreciation.

***Haughty*** : *adj.* aloof, proud, prideful, arrogant; *Ant.* humble, simple, down-to-earth, unaffected.

***Hazardous*** : *adj.* perilous, dangerous, risky; *Ant.* safe, secure.

***Headstrong*** : *adj.* stubborn, obstinate, willful; *Ant.* amenable, easygoing.

***Healthy*** : *adj.* hale, hearty, robust, vigorous, strong, sound, healthful; *Ant.* unhealthy, ill, sick, unwholesome.

***Heat*** : *n.* 1. warmth, hotness, temperature; 2. passion, excitement; 3. warmth, zeal, ardour; *vb.* warm, inflame, cook; *Ant. n.* 1. coolness, cold, coldness, iciness, chilliness. *vb.* cool, freeze, chill.

***Heavy*** : *adj.* 1. weighty, ponderous; 2. intense, concentrated, severe; 3. burdensome, oppressive, harsh, depressing; 4. sad, oppressed, serious, grave, gloomy, mournful, melancholy, dismal; 5. boring, dull, tiresome; *Ant.* 1. light, buoyant; airy. 2. light, insignificant, minimal. 3. cheerful, happy.

***Heed*** : *vb.* obey, regard, observe; *n.* attention, mind; *Ant. vb.* ignore, disregard, overlook, disdain.

***Height*** : *n.* 1. altitude, elevation, tallness, 2. mountain, peak, prominence; 3. acme, pinnacle, maximum; *Ant.* depth.

***Helpful*** : *adj.* advantageous, profitable, valuable; *Ant.* useless, futile, worthless.

***Helpless*** : *adj.* 1. dependent, feeble, weak, disabled; 2. unresourceful, incompetent, inept, incapable; *Ant.* competent, resourceful, enterprising.

***Heroic*** : *adj.* valiant, brave, valorous, dauntless, gallant, courageous, bold, fearless; *Ant.* cowardly, fainthearted, timid.

***Heroism*** : *n.* bravery, valour, gallantry, courage, boldness; *Ant.* cowardice, uncourageousness, timidity.

***Hesitate*** : *vb.* pause, wait, delay; *Ant.* proceed.

***Hide*** : *vb.* conceal, cover, mask, screen, camouflage, cloak, shroud, veil; *n.* skin, pelt, leather, fur; *Ant. vb.* show, display, reveal.

***Hideous*** : *adj.* ugly, frightful, frightening, shocking, horrible, horrifying, terrible, terrifying, monstrous, gross, grisly; *Ant.* beautiful, lovely, ethereal, beauteous.

***High*** : *adj.* 1. tall, lofty, towering; 2. raised, shrill, high-pitched, strident, sharp; 3. important, prominent, powerful; 4. dear, expansive, costly, high-priced; 5. serious, grave, extreme; *Ant.* 1. low, short, lowly; 2. deep; 3. lowly, unimportant, insignificant; 4. reasonable, inexpensive; 5. petty, trivial.

***Hinder*** : *vb.* interrupt, hamper, slow, delay, obstruct, interfere with, block, thwart, prevent, stop; *Ant.* advance, further, promote.

***Hire*** : *vb.* 1. employ, engage, retain, enlist; 2. rent, lease, charter; *n.* rent, rental, lease, let, charter; *Ant.* 1. dismiss, fire.

***Hoard*** : *vb.* amass, save, store, secrete; *n.* store, stock, cache; *Ant. vb.* spend, use, squander.

***Hoarse*** : *adj.* rough, raucous, deep, husky, grating, harsh; *Ant.* clear.

***Hollow*** : *adj.* 1. vacant, empty, unfilled; 2. empty, false, flimsy, meaningless; *n.* cavity, hole, depression, pit; *vb.* excavate, dig, shovel; *Ant. adj.* 1. full, filled, solid.

***Holy*** : *adj.* 1. blessed, sacred, hollowed, consecrated; 2. saintly, sainted, divine, pious; *Ant.* 1. profane, unconsecrated, unsanctified.

***Homely*** : *adj.* plain, unattractive, ugly; *Ant.* attractive, beautiful, handsome, comely, pretty.

***Honest*** : *adj.* 1. truthful, trustworthy, moral, upright, honourable; 2. open, candid, forthright, frank, straightforward; *Ant.* 1. dishonest, fraudulent.

***Honesty*** : *n.* 1. integrity, uprightness, trustworthiness. fairness, honour; 2. candour, frankness, sincerity; *Ant.* 1. dishonesty, fraud.

***Honour*** : *n.* 1. respect, esteem, distinction; 2. principle, character, honesty, uprightness; *vb.* 1. respect, esteem; 2. admire, revere; 3. accept, acknowledge, clear; *Ant.* *n.* 1. dishonour, disgrace, shame; *vb.* 1. dishonour, disgrace, shame.

***Honourable*** : *adj.* 1. honest, noble, just, fair; 2. illustrious, famed, distinguished; *Ant.* 1. dishonourable, shameful, humiliating.

***Hope*** : *n.* 1. expectation, anticipation; 2. trust, faith, confidence; *vb.* desire, aspire, expect; *Ant.* *n.* 2. hopelessness, despair.

***Hopeful*** : *adj.* confident, optimistic; *Ant.* hopeless, despairing; pessimistic.

***Hopeless*** : *adj.* 1. despairing, desperate, forlorn; 2. incurable, fatal, disastrous; *Ant.* hopeful, promising.

***Horizontal*** : *adj.* 1. level, even, plane, flat, straight; 2. sideways; *Ant.* vertical, upright.

***Horrible*** : *adj.* horrifying, awful, terrible, horrid, dreadful, ghastly; *Ant.* wonderful splendid.

***Hostile*** : *adj.* unfriendly, antagonistic, warlike; *Ant.* friendly, hospitable.

***Hot*** : *adj.* 1. torrid, heated, burning, fiery, blazing, sizzling, roasting, frying, broiling, boiling, scorching, searing; 2. spicy, sharp, biting; 3. excited, violent, passionate, ardent; *Ant.* 1. cold, cool, chilly, freezing. 2. bland, tasteless.

***Hotheaded*** : *adj.* reckless, rash, unruly, touchy, testy, short-tempered, irritable; *Ant.* coolheaded, levelheaded calm.

***Huge*** : *adj.* enormous, gigantic, immense, colossal, tremendous; large, big; *Ant.* small, tiny, diminutive, miniature.

***Humane*** : *adj.* kind, thoughtful, kindly, merciful, kindhearted, tender, gentle, softhearted; *Ant.* cruel, mean, heartless.

***Humble*** : *adj.* 1. unassuming, modest, unpretending, unpretentious; 2. polite, courteous, respectful; *vb.* lower, reduce, degrade, downgrade, shame; *Ant. adj.* 1, vain, proud, haughty.

***Humorous*** : *adj.* funny, comical, comic, amusing; *Ant.* serious, unfunny, sobre, sombre.

***Hungry*** : *adj.* famished, starved; *Ant.* full, sated, glutted.

***Hurry*** : *vb.* 1. rush, run, speed, race, hasten; 2. rush, hasten, urge, accelerate; *n.* rush, haste, bustle, ado; *Ant. vb.* 1. linger, tarry, dawdle.

# I

***Idiotic*** : *adj.* stupid, senseless, foolish, inane, moronic, halfwitted, thimble-witted, simpleminded, dimwitted; *Ant.* intelligent, bright, brilliant, smart.

***Idle*** : *adj.* 1. unemployed, inactive, unoccupied, unused; 2. lazy, sluggish; *Ant.* 1. active, busy, occupied, engaged.

***Ignorant*** : *adj.* 1. untrained, uneducated, illiterate, untaught; 2. unaware, unmindful, unwiting, uninformed; *Ant.* 1. educated, cultivated, cultured, schooled, lettered, learned; 2. aware, informed.

***Ignore*** : *vb.* disregard, overlook, omit, neglect; *Ant.* notice.

***Ill*** : *adj.* sick, unwell, unhealthy, diseased, ailing; *Ant.* well, healthy, fit.

***Illegal*** : *adj.* unlawful, illicit; *Ant.* legal, lawful, legitimate.

***Illuminate*** : *vb.* 1. light, light up, brighten, lighten; 2. enlighten, explain, clarify, interpret; *Ant.* 1. darken, shadow, becloud, obscure.

***llusion*** : *n.* mirage, delusion, hallucination, vision, fantasy; *Ant.* reality, actuality.

***Imaginary*** : *adj.* unreal, fanciful, whimsical, fanctastic; *Ant.* real, actual.

***Immediate*** : *adj.* 1. instant, instantaneous, present; 2. near, next, close prompt; 3. direct *Ant.* 1. long-range, distant. 2. future.

***Immense*** : *adj.* huge, enormous, vast, gigantic, great, large, big; *Ant.* small, tiny, minuscule, petite.

***Impertinent*** : *adj.* impudent, insolent, rude, disrespectful; *Ant.* polite, courteous, respectful.

***Impetuous*** : *adj.* rash hasty, impulsive; *Ant.* careful, cautious, thoughtful, prudent.

***Imply*** : *vb.* hint, suggest, indicate, mention; *Ant.* state, declare.

***Impolite*** : *adj.* rude, unpleasant, discourteous, insolent, impertinent, uncivil; *Ant.* polite, courteous, respectful.

***Important*** : *adj.* 1. essential, significant, considerable, primary, principal; 2. famed, illustrious, well-known, famous, distinguished, notable; *Ant.* 1. unimportant, trivial, trifling, secondary; 2. inconsequential, anonymous.

***Improper*** : *adj.* 1. unsuitable, unfit, inappropriate; 2. indecent, naughty, unbecoming; *Ant.* proper, fitting appropriate.

***Improve*** : *vb.* better, refine, upgrade; *Ant.* impair.

***Impudent*** : *adj.* impertinent, fresh, insolent, insulting, rude; *Ant.* courteous, polite, respectful.

***Impulsive*** : *adj.* hasty, rash; spontaneous, automatic; *Ant.* careful, cautious, prudent.

***Inaccurate*** : *adj.* incorrect, wrong, mistaken, faulty; *Ant.* accurate, correct, right.

***Incentive*** : *n.* inducement, stimulus, impulse, encouragement; *Ant.* discouragement.

***Incessant*** : *adj.* unending, eternal, continuous, perpetual, constant, relentless; *Ant.* intermittent, irregular, spasmodic.

***Incidental*** : *adj.* secondary, unimportant, trivial; *Ant.* fundamental, basic.

***Inclination*** : *n.* 1. tendency, predisposition, preference, prejudice ; 2. slope, slant, incline, lean; *Ant.* 1. disinclination, reluctance. 2. uprightness, straightness.

***Incline*** : *vb.* lean, slope, nod; *Ant.* straighten.

***Include*** : *vb.* embrace, encompass, contain, involve; *Ant.* exclude, omit.

***Income*** : *n.* salary, earnings, wages, pay, revenue, receipts, return; *Ant.* expense.

***Incompetent*** : *adj.* unfit, incapable, unqualified; clumsy, awakward; *Ant.* competent, able, skilled.

***Inconvenient*** : *adj.* inappropriate, awkward, troublesome, untimely; *Ant.* convenient, handy.

***Incorrect*** : *adj.* wrong, inaccurate, mistaken erroneous; *Ant.* accurate, proper, suitable.

***Increase*** : *vb.* swell, enlarge, greaten, extend, grow, prolong, lengthen, broden; *Ant. vb.* decrease, shrink, lessen, diminish. *n.* decrease, lessening, shrinkage.

***Incredible*** : *adj.* unbelievable, improbable; *Ant.* credible, plausible, believable.

***Indefinite*** : *adj.* uncertain, unsure, vague, unsettled, confused, confusing; *Ant.* definite, decided, unequivocal.

***Independence*** : *n.* liberty, freedom; *Ant.* dependence, reliance.

***Indifferent*** : *adj.* unconcerned, uncaring, cool, insensitive, nonchalant; *Ant.* concerned, caring, earnest.

***Indignant*** : *adj.* angry, irritated, aroused, exasperated, irate; *Ant.* serene, calm, content.

***Indolent*** : *adj.* lazy, idle, slow, sluggish, inactive; *Ant.* vigorous, active, dynamic, zestful.

***Induce*** : *vb.* persuade, influence, convience; *Ant.* dissuade, discourage.

***Inducement*** : *n.* lure, entirement, incentive, stimulus; *Ant.* discouragement.

***Industrious*** : *adj.* hard-working, busy, diligent, persistent; *Ant.* lazy, indolent, shiftless.

***Inexpensive*** : *adj.* low-priced, modest, economical; cheap; *Ant.* expensive, costly, dear.

***Inexperienced*** : *adj.* untrained, green; uninformed, naive; *Ant.* skilled, experienced, seasoned, trained, sophisticated.

***Infantile*** : *adj.* childish, immature, babyish, naive; *Ant.* grown-up, mature, adult.

***Inferior*** : *adj.* lower, second-rate, medicore; *Ant.* superior higher.

***Infinite*** : *adj.* vast, boundless, innumerable, numberless, endless, unlimited, limitless; *Ant.* finite, limited.

***Inflame*** : *vb.* excite, arouse, incite, fire; *Ant.* calm, soothe.

***Inflate*** : *vb.* swell, expand, blow up, distend; *Ant.* deflate, collapse.

***Inflexible*** : *adj.* rigid, unbending, firm, unyielding, immovable, steadfast; *Ant.* flexible, pliant, yielding, giving, elastic.

***Initial*** : *adj.* first, basic, primary, elementary; *Ant.* last, final, terminal.

***Initiate*** : *vb.* start, commence, open; *Ant.* stop, finish, terminate.

***Injurious*** : *adj.* harmful, hurtful, damaging, destructive; *Ant.* beneficial, useful, advantgeous.

***Innocent*** : *adj.* 1. not guilty, blameless, faultless, virtuous; 2. unknowning, naive, unsophisticated; *Ant.* 1. guilty, blameworthy. 2. sophisticated, wise, worldly.

***Inquisitive*** : *adj.* inquiring, questioning, prying, curious; *Ant.* uninterested, incurious.

***Insane*** : *adj.* deranged, lunatic, demented, mentally unsound, mad, crazy; 2. senseless, foolish, stupid, idiotic; *Ant.* 1. sane, coherent, rational.

***Insolent*** : *adj.* impertinent, rude, disrespectful, insulting; *Ant.* polite, courteous, respectful.

***Insult*** : *vb.* offend, outrage, humilitate; *n.* offense, affront, outrage, scorn; *Ant. vb.* flatter, praise; *n.* flattery, praise.

***Integrated*** : *adj.* combined, interspersed, mingled, mixed; desegrated, inter-racial, non sectarian; *Ant.* segregated, separated, divided.

***Intelligent*** : *adj.* smart, bright, clever, quick, astute, alert, wise; *Ant.* stupid, slow, unintelligent, dumb.

***Intentional*** : *adj.* purposeful, deliberate, planned, intended; *Ant.* accidental, chance.

***Intentionally*** : *adv.* purposefully, on purpose, deliberately; maliciously; *Ant.* accidentally.

***Interest*** : *n.* 1. concern, care, attention; 2. profit, advantage, benefit, gain; 3. share, ownership, credit; 4. percentage, premium; *vb.* 1. attract, engage, absorb; 2. entertain, amuse, engage; *Ant. n.* 1. disinterest, apathy; *vb.* 1. bore, weary.

***Interested*** : *adj.* concerned, involved, affected; *Ant.* uninterested, unconcerned, indifferent.

***Interesting*** : *adj.* attractive, fascinating, engaging, inviting; *Ant.* uninteresting, boring, tedious, wearisome.

***Interior*** : *n.* inside, centre; *Adj.* inside, central, inner, internal; *Ant. n.* exterior, outside; *Adj.* external, outer, outside..

***Internal*** : *adj.* 1. inner, interior, inside, private, intimate; 2. domestic, native; *Ant.* external, outer, surface.

***Intolerant*** : *adj.* prejudiced, biased, bigoted; *Ant.* tolerant, broadminded, fair.

***Inviting*** : *adj.* alluring, luring, appealing, tempting, attractive, encouraging; *Ant.* uninviting, unattractive.

***Involuntary*** : *adj.* automatic, reflex, uncontrolled; unintentional; *Ant.* voluntary, willed, willful.

***Irregular*** : *adj.* 1. uneven, unequal, crooked; 2. disorderly, random, unsettled, disorganised; *Ant.* 1. regular, even.

***Irritate*** : *vb.* 1. annoy, vex, pester, bother; 2. redden, chafe, inflame; *Ant.* 1. soothe, pacify, calm.

***Irritable*** : *adj.* sensitive, touchy, testy, peevish, short-tempered. fretful; *Ant.* cheerful, happy.

# J

***Join*** : *vb.* unite, connect, couple, assemble, link, fit, attach; *Ant.* split, separate, divide, sunder.

***Joint*** : *n.* connection, link, coupling, union, junction; *adj.* common, mutual, combined, connected; *Ant. adj.* separate, divided.

***Jolly*** : *adj.* joyful, gleeful, gay, spirted, happy, cheerful, glad; *Ant.* sad, sombre, gloomy, melancholy.

***Joy*** : *n.* delight, pleasure, happiness, gladness, satisfaction; *Ant.* unhappiness, misery, sadness, gloom.

***Jumpy*** : *adj.* nervous, touchy, sensltive, excitable; *Ant.* calm, tranquil, unruffled.

# K

***Keen*** : *adj.* 1. sharp, acute; 2. quick, shrewd, bright, clever, intelligent; 3. enthusiastic, eager, interested; *Ant.* 1. dull, blunted; 2. dull, stupid, slow, obtuse.

***Kind*** : *adj.* friendly, gentle, kindly, mild, kindhearted, goodhearted, warm, tender, affectionate; *Ant.* cruel, brutal, mean, hardhearted.

***Kingly*** : *adj.* regal, kinglike, royal, majestic, imperial; *Ant.* lowly, squalid.

# L

***Laborious*** : *adj.* 1. difficult, tiring, burdensome, hard; 2. painstaking, industrious; *Ant.* 1. easy, simple, restful, relaxing.

***Lack*** : *n.* shortage, need, dearth, want, scarcity; *vb.* want, need, require; *Ant. n.* abundance, quantity, plentifulness, profusion.

***Lame*** : *adj.* 1. crippled, disabled, limping; deformed; 2. poor, unsatisfactory, weak, inadequate, faulty; *Ant.* 2. convincing, believable, plausible.

***Large*** : *adj.* big, great, sizeable, broad, massive, huge, vast, enormous, immense; *Ant.* small, little, tiny, diminutive.

***Last*** : *adj.* final, latest, ultimate, extrème, concluding; *vb.* continue, remain, endure; *Ant. adj.* first, initial, starting, beginning.

***Launch*** : *vb.* 1. fire, drive, propel; 2. initiate, originate, start, begin; *Ant.* 2. stop, finish, terminate.

***Lawless*** : *adj.* uncontrolled, uncivilised, wild, untamed, savage, violent; *Ant.* law-abiding, obedient, tame.

***Lazy*** : *adj.* indolent, slothful, idle, inactive, sluggish; *Ant.*

ambitious, active, forceful, go-getting.

***Lead*** : *vb.* 1. guide, conduct, direct, steer; 2. command, direct; *Ant.* follow.

***Leader*** : *n.* director, chief, commander, head, manager, ruler; *Ant.* follower, disciple.

***Lean*** : *adj.* slender, slim, thin, lanky, gaunt, skinny; *n.* meat, sinew, muscle; *Ant. adj.* fat, porty, heavy, obese.

***Learned*** : *adj.* scholarly, wise, educated, knowledgeable, well-informed; *Ant.* ignorant, uneducated, unlettered, illiterate.

***Least*** : *adj.* 1. smallest, tiniest, minutest; 2. slightest; trivial, *Ant.* 1. most.

***Leave*** : *vb.* 1. depart, go, quit, desert, abandon; 2. bequeath, will; *n.* 1. permission, allowance, liberty, freedom, consent; 2. furlough, vacation, holiday; *Ant. vb.* 1. arrive, come.

***Legal*** : *adj.* lawful, legtimate, honest; *Ant. adj.* illegal, illegitimate, unlawful.

***Lengthen*** : *vb.* extend, stretch, reach, prolong, grow, increase; *Ant.* shorten, contract, shrink.

***Lessen*** : *vb.* reduce, diminish, decrease, shrink, dwindle, decline; *Ant.* increase, swell, expand, multiply.

***Liberal*** : *adj.* 1. generous, openhanded, unselfish, kind; 2. tolerant, unprejudiced, unbigoted, openminded; *Ant.* 1. stingy, cheap, tightfisted, selfish.

***Liberate*** : *vb.* free, release, loose, deliver; *Ant.* imprison, confine, jail.

***Liberty*** : *n.* freedom, independence; *Ant.* bondage, servitude, slavery.

***Light*** : *n.* 1. illumination, radiance, brilliance, brightness; 2. lamp, fixture, chandelier, candle, bulb; *vb.* 1. illuminate, brighten; 2. ignite, fire, burn, kindle; *adj.* 1.

bright, clear, luminous, lit, illuminated; 2. pale, whitish, bleached; *Ant. n.* dark. *vb.* 1. darken; 2. extinguish; *adj.* dark.

***Light*** : *adj.* 1. unsubstantial, airy, buyoant, dainty; 2. giddy, frivolous 3. trivial, shallow, slight; 3. serious, heavy, weighty; *Ant.* substantial, concrete, earthy, stolid; 2. serious; sombre.

***Lightheaded*** : *adj.* silly, frivolous, giddy, dizzy; *Ant.* clearheaded, sober, rational.

***Lighthearted*** : *adj.* gay, carefree, cheerful, merry, happy, glad; *Ant.* sad, melancholy, sombre, serious; *vb.* admire, esteem, fancy, care for, cherish, adore, love; *Ant.* dislike, disapprove, hate, loathe.

***Liking*** : *n.* affection, partiality, fondness; *Ant.* dislike, antipathy.

***Literate*** : *adj.* educated, informed intelligent; *Ant.* illiterate, unread, unlettered ignorant.

***Little*** : *adj.* 1. small, tiny, wee, minute; 2. brief, short; *adv.* slightly; *Ant. adj.* 1. larg, big, huge; 2. long, extended.

***Lively*** : *adj.* 1. active, live, vigorous, spry, nimble, quick; 2. gay, animated, spirited; *Ant.* slow, dull, sluggish.

***Lofty*** : *adj.* 1. tall, high, towering; 2. exalted, elevated; 3. proud, scornful, haughty; *Ant.* 1. lowly, low.

***Logical*** : *adj.* reasonable, rational, sensible; *Ant.* irrational, crazy.

***Long*** : *adj.* extensive, lengthy, extended; *Ant.* short, brief, limited.

***Long-winded*** : *adj.* dull, boring; wordy; *Ant.* terse, curt.

***Loose*** : *adj.* 1. unfastened, united, free, undone; 2. wobbly, insecure, unscrewed, movable; 3. baggy, draped, slack; *vb.* loosen; set free; *Ant. adj.* 1. fastened, tied, secure; 2. firm, secure, steady; 3. tight, confining.

***Lovely*** : *adj.* attractive, fair, charming, comely, pretty, beautiful, handsome; *Ant.* homely, ugly, hideous.

***Lower*** : *vb.* 1. reduce, decrease, lessen, diminish; 2. soften, quiet, turn down; 3. degrade, disgrace, humble; 4. sink, drop; *Ant.* 1., 2., 4. increase, raise.

***Loyal*** : *adj.* faithfully, true, devoted, dependable, patriotic; *Ant.* disloyal, treacherous, traitorous.

***Loyalty*** : *n.* faithfulness, devotion, fidelity; allegiance, patriotism; *Ant.* disloyalty, treachery, traitorousness.

***Luck*** : *n.* fortune, chance, fluke; *Ant.* misfortune.

***Lucky*** : *adj.* fortunate, favourable, favoured, blessed; *Ant.* unlucky, unfortunate.

***Luxurious*** : *adj.* lavish, rich, splendid, deluxe; *Ant.* sparse, Spartan, simple, crude.

# M

***Mad*** : *adj.* 1. insane, crazy, mentally ill, deranged; 2. angry, furious, energed, irate, raging; *Ant.* 1. sane, rational lucid; 2. happy, cheerful, content.

***Madden*** : *vb.* enrage, infuriate, anger, vex, annoy; *Ant.* mollify, calm, please.

***Magnificent*** : *adj.* 1. splendid, luxurious, rich, lavish, grand; 2. marvellous, wonderful, extraordinary, impressive; pliant, plain, simple.

***Magnify*** : *vb.* enlarge, increase; *Ant.* diminish, reduce.

***Main*** : *adj.* chief, principal, foremost; *Ant.* secondary, accessory.

***Maintain*** : *vb.* 1. keep, continue, keep up, preserve, support; 2. preserve, keep, keep up, renew; 3. assert, state, hold, declare, claim, contend; *Ant.* 1. discontinue.

***Majestic*** : *adj.* 1. royal, kingly, princely, regal, noble, grand, stately; *Ant.* 1. lowly, base; 2. squalid.

***Major*** : *adj.* greater, larger, important, chief; *Ant.* minor, inconsequential.

***Male*** : *adj.* masculine, mainly, virile; *Ant.* female, feminine, womanly.

***Malice*** : *n.* spite, resentment, viciousness, grudge, bitterness; *Ant.* benevolence, charity.

***Mammoth*** : *adj.* huge, colossal, enormous, immense, elephantine, gigantic; *Ant.* small, tiny, minuscule.

***Manage*** : *vb.* 1. direct, ginde, lead, supervise, superintend, control, conduct, administer, rule; 2. succeed, arrange, bring about; 3. handle, control, manipulate; *Ant.* 1. mismanage, bungle.

***Manageable*** : *adj.* controllable, docile, tractable, willing, obedient; *Ant.* unmanageable wild, recalcitrant.

***Many*** : *adj.* numerous, abundant, plentiful; *Ant.* few.

***Marriage*** : *n.* 1. wedding, nuptials; 2. matrimony, wedlock; union 3. alliance, association,conferation;*Ant.* divorce. separation.

***Marvellous*** : *adj.* wonderful, miraculous, wondrous, extraordinary, amazing, astonishing, astounding; *Ant.* commonplace, ordinary, usual.

***Masculine*** : *adj.* 1. male; 2. manly, brave, bold, courageous; *Ant.* feminine, female, unmasculine.

***Massive*** : *adj.* 1. huge, immense, gigantic, tremendous; 2. large, bulky, weighty, ponderous; *Ant.* 1. small, little, tiny; 2. light, weightless.

***Masterly*** : *adj.* skilful, expert, superb, adroit; *Ant.* clumsy, maladroit, awkward.

***Matchless*** : *adj.* unequalled, unrivalled, peerless, incomparable; *Ant.* unimpressive, ordinary.

***Material*** : *n.* 1. substance, matter, stuff; fabric; 2. cloth, fabric, textile; *adj.* 1. substantial, considerable, important; 2. physical, real, touchable, palapable, tangible; *Ant. adj.* 1. immaterial, irrelevant; 2. immaterial, intangible, spiritual.

***Mature*** : *adj.* 1. ripe, aged, ready, seasoned; 2. adult, full-grown, matured, grown; *vb.* age, ripen, develop; *Ant.*

*adj.* 1. young, youthful. 2. immature, innocent, naive.

***Meagre*** : *adj.* scantly, sparse, frugal, mean; *Ant.* plentiful, bountiful, ample, abundant.

***Mean*** : *adj.* 1. unkind, cruel, nasty, rude; 2. stingry miserly, tight, selfish; *Ant.* 1. gentle, thoughtful, kind 2. generous, openhanded.

***Measureless*** : *adj.* limitless, immeasurable, boundless, immense, vast, infinite; *Ant.* measurable, ascertainable, figurable.

***Medium*** : *n.* 1. average modicum, 2. means, mechanism, factor; *adj.* average, median, middling; *Ant. n.* extreme.

***Meet*** : *vb.* 1. encounter, come across *or* upon; 2. converage, connect, join, unite; 3. settle, satisfy, fulfil, answer, discharge; 4. convene, gather, assemble, congregate; 5. agree, unite *n.* contest, meeting, competition, match; *Ant. vb.* 1. miss; 2. diverage, split; 4. scatter; 5. disagree.

***Melancholy*** : *n.* sadness, gloom, depression; *adj.* sad, gloomy, depressed, downcast, downhearted, blue, unhappy; *Ant. adj.* happy joyful, jubilant.

***Mellow*** : *adj.* 1. ripe, mature, cured, aged, full-flavoured; 2. smooth sweet, melodius; *vb.* ripen, mature, develop, soften; *Ant. adj.* 1. immature, unripened.

***Melt*** : *vb.* 1. liquefy, dissolve; 2. fade out, blend, dwindle, vanish, disappear; 3. soften, relax; *Ant.* 1. harden, freeze, solidify.

***Memorable*** : *adj.* historic, unforgettable, important, significant; *Ant.* forgettable, passing, transitory.

***Mend*** : *vb.* 1. repair, patch, restore, fix; 2. improve, recover, recuperate, heal; *Ant.* 1. ruin, destroy, spoil.

***Mental*** : *adj.* intellectual, reasoning, thinking; *Ant.* physical.

***Merciful*** : *adj.* kind, compassionate, lenient, forgiving tenderhearted, kindhearted, sympathetic; unjust, unforgiving, harsh, mean, vengeful.

***Merciless*** : *adj.* cruel, ruthless, pitiless, savage, hard, hardhearted, unfeeling; *Ant.* merciful, benevolent, openhearted.

***Mercy*** : *n.* 1. compassion, sympathy, pity, consideration, leniency, kindness, pity, tenderness; 2. disposal, discretion, disposition; *Ant.* 1. cruelty, ruthlessness, pitlessness.

***Mere*** : *adj.* bare, scant; *Ant.* considerable, substantial

***Merry*** : *adj.* cheerful, cheerful, joyful, gay, happy, jolly, joyous, jovial; *Ant.* sad, doleful, gloomy.

***Messy*** : *adj.* dirty, disorderly, disordered, confused, confusing untidy, sloppy, slovenly; *Ant.* neat, orderly, tidy.

***Middle*** : *n.* centre, midpoint, median; *adj.* centre, central halfway, intermediate; *Ant. n. adj.* beginning, end.

***Might*** : *n.* power, strength, force; *Ant.* weakness, frailty, vulnerability.

***Mighty*** : *adj.* strong, powerful, muscular; *Ant.* weak, frail.

***Migrate*** : *vb.* move resettle; immigrate, emigrate; *Ant.* remain, stay, settle.

***Mild*** : *adj.* 1. claim, gentle, temperate, pleasant; 2. amiable, kind, compassionate, peaceful, calm; 3. bland, soothing; *Ant.* 1. stormy, turbulent; 2. violent, excitable, hottempered.

***Mingle*** : *vb.* combine, mix, blend; *Ant.* separate, sort.

***Miniature*** : *adj.* tiny, small, midget, little minute; *Ant.* outsize.

***Minimize*** : *vb.* diminish, decrease, lessen, reduce; *Ant.* maximise, enlarge.

***Minor*** : *adj.* smaller, lesser, secondary, petty, unimportant; *n.* boy, girl, child, youth, adolescent; *Ant. adj.* major *n.* adult, grown-up.

***Minute*** : *adj.* tiny, wee, microscopic, minuscule; *Ant.* large, huge, immense.

***Miraculous*** : *adj.* marvellous, wonderful, incredible, phenomenal, extraordinary; *Ant.* ordinary, commonplace, everyday.

***Mirth*** : *n.* glee, joy, gaiety, joyousness, jollity, joyfulness, merriment, laughter; *Ant.* gloom, sadness, seriousness.

***Miscarry*** : *vb.* fail, go wrong; *Ant.* succeed.

***Mischievous*** : *adj.* prankish, rougish, playful, naughty, *Ant.* good, well-behaved.

***Miser*** : *n.* skinflint, tighwad, scrooge: *Ant.* philianthropist.

***Miserable*** : *adj.* 1. unhappy, uncomfortable, wretched, heartbroken; 2. poor, penniless, needy, poverty-stricken; 3. mean, contemptible, hatful, low, wretched, bad; 4. unlucky, unfortunate, luckless; *Ant.* 1. happy, joyful, content; 2. wealthy, well-off, prosperous; 3. noble, honourable; 4. lucky, fortunate.

***Miserly*** : *adj.* stingy, tightfisted, pennypinching, cheap, mean, selfish, *Ant.* generous, openhanded, spendthrift, extravagant.

***Misery*** : *n.* 1. unhappiness, suffering, anguish, woe, agony, distress; 2. grief, sorrow; *Ant.* 1. delight, joy.

***Mistaken*** : *adj.* wrong, incorrect, confused, misinformed, inaccurate; *Ant.* correct, right, accurate.

***Misunderstand*** : *vb.* misinterpret, misjudge, confuse, jumble, mistake; *Ant.* comprehend, perceive.

***Mix*** : *vb.* combine, blend, mingle; *n.* combination, blend, mixture; *Ant. vb.* separate, divide.

***Mobile*** : *adj.* movable, free, portable; *Ant.* immobile, stationary, fixed mock *vb.* scorn, deride, ridicule, tease, jeer; *adj.* imitation fake franhulent sham; *Ant. vb.* praise, honour, applaud; *adj.* real, genuine, authentic.

***Mockery*** : *n.* 1. ridicule, scorn, derision; *Ant.* 2. travesty, sham, pretext, pretence; *Ant.* praise, admiration.

***Moderate*** : *adj.* reasonable, average, medium, fair; 2. conservative, middle-of-the-road, cautious; *Ant.* 1. immoderate, excessive, heavy.

***Moderate*** : *vb.* 1. arbitrate, referee, judge, umpire; 2. weaken, pacify, lessen, calm, sober, temper; *Ant.* 2. intensify, increase, aggravate.

***Modern*** : *adj.* present-day, up-to-date, recent, novel, new, fresh, modish, stylish; *Ant.* old-fashioned, antique, out-of-date, outmoded.

***Modest*** : *adj.* 1. demure, decent, prudish; 2. humble, moderate, proper, unassuming, retiring, humble, simple, plain; *Ant.* 1. immodest, libertine, loose; 2. gaudy, outlandish, tasteless, showy; 3. vain, proud, arrogant, modesty; *n.* humility, simplicity, decency, propriety; *Ant.* vanity, conceit, pride.

***Moist*** : *adj.* damp, dank, humid, muggy, clammy, wet; *Ant.* dry, arid, parched.

***Moisten*** : *vb.* dampen; wet; *Ant.* dry.

***Moisture*** : *n.* dampness, wetness, condensation, mist; *Ant.* dryness, aridity.

***Momentous*** : *adj.* important, serious, consequential, essential; *Ant.* unimportant, trivial, trifling.

***Monotonous*** : *adj.* boring, dull, tedious, humdrum, tiring, tiresome, wearisome; *Ant.* interesting, fascinating, riveting.

***Monstrous*** : *adj.* 1. huge, tremendous, immense, gigantic, enormous; 2. horrible, revolting, shocking repulsive, hideous, dreadful, terrible; *Ant.* 1. tiny, diminutive, small, miniature.

***Monumental*** : *adj.* 1. huge, enormous, immense, colossal, gigantic; 2. significant, important; *Ant.* 1. miniature, tiny. 2. insignificant, trivial.

***Moody*** : *adj.* temperamental, changeable, short-tempered, irritable testy, peevish, fretful, spiteful; *Ant:* calm, even-tempered, good-natured.

***Moral*** : *adj.* upright, honest, ethical, just, good, honourable; *Ant.* immoral, dishonest, sinful, corrupt.

***Motion*** : *n.* movement, change, action; *vb.* gesture, signal, indicate; *Ant. n.* stillness, immobility.

***Mount*** : *vb.* 1. ascend, climb, go up; 2. rise, increase, ascend; 3. prepare, make ready, ready set up; *n.* 1. horse, steed, charger; 2. mountain; hill; *Ant. vb.* 1., 2. descend.

***Mourn*** : *vb.* lament, grieve, sorrow, bemoan; *Ant.* rejoice, celebrate.

***Mournful*** : *adj.* sad, sorrowful; *Ant.* cheerful, joyful, happy.

***Muffle*** : *vb.* deaden, soften, quiet, mute; *Ant.* amplify, louden.

***Multiply*** : *vb.* 1. increase; double, triple, treble; 2. reproduce, propagate; *Ant.* decrease, lessen.

***Mutinous*** : *adj.* rebellious, revolutionary, unruly; *Ant.* obedient, dutiful, compliant.

***Mysterious*** : *adj.* secret, puzzling strange; *Ant.* open, direct, obvious.

# N

***Naked*** : *adj.* 1. unclothed, underssed, bare, uncovered, nude; 2. simple, plain, obvious, unadorned, undisguised; *Ant.* 1. covered, clothed, garbed; 2. suppressed, concealed.

***Narrow*** : *adj.* 1. slender, thin, tapering, tapered, tight; 2. close, precarious, perilous, dangerous; *Ant.* 1. wide, broad.

***Narrow-minded*** : *adj.* intolerant, closed, bigoted, close-minded, prejudiced, biased; *Ant.* broad-minded, liberal, tolerant.

***Nasty*** : *adj.* 1. disagreeable, unpleasant, foul; 2. dirty, filthy, foul, disgusting, loathsome, polluted, offensive; 3. dirty, foul, filthy, obscence, indecent, improper; 4. disagreeable, cranky, unpleasant, vicious, ugly; *Ant.* 1. pleasant, fair, seasonable; 2. clean, pure; 3. proper, decent; 4. pleasant, even-tempered.

***Native*** : *adj.* 1. natural, innate, inborn, inbred, hereditary; 2. local, original; *n.* national, citizen, inhabitant, resident; *Ant. adj.* 2. foreign, alien; *n.* stranger, foreigner, outsider.

***Natural*** : *adj.* 1. inbred, inborn, innate, inherited, hereditary, original, basic, fundamental; 2. normal, customary, typical, usual; characteristic; *Ant.* unnatural, alien, contrary.

***Naturally*** : *adv.* 1. normally, usually, typically, ordinarily, customarily; 2. freely, readily, simply, openly, sincerely; *Ant.* 2. artifically.

***Naughty*** : *adj.* 1. disobedient, unruly, unmanageable, insubordinate, mischievous; 2. indecent, improper, rude; *Ant.* 1. good, well-behaved, obedient.

***Near*** : *adj.* close, nearby, neighbouring, adjoining; *Ant.* far, distant, remote.

***Neat*** : *adj.* 1. clean, orderly, tidy, trim, dapper, natty, smart, elegant; 2. orderly, well-organised; *Ant.* 1. messy, sloppy, unkempt, disorganised.

***Necessary*** : *adj.* needed, required, important, essential; *Ant.* unnecessary, dispensable, unneeded.

***Needy*** : *adj.* poor, poverty-stricken, penniless, destitute; *Ant.* wealthy, well-to-do, affluent, well-off, well heeled.

***Neglect*** : *vb.* 1. disregard, overlook, ignore; 2. omit, skip, miss; *n.* disregard, negligence, inattention; *Ant. vb.* 1. care, attend, *n.* attention, concern, regard.

***Nerve*** : *n.* 1. courage, boldness, bravery, spirit; 2. effrontery, impudence, rudeness, impertinence; *Ant.* 1. cowardice, weakness, frailty.

***Nervous*** : *adj.* 1. restless, excited, agitated; 2. timid, shy, fearful; *Ant.* 1. calm, tranquil, placid; 2. bold, courageous, confident.

***Neautral*** : *adj.* 1. uninvolved, inactive, non-partisan; 2. dull, drab; *Ant.* 1. partisan, biased.

***New*** : *adj.* 1. novel, fresh, unique, original, unusal; 2. recent, modern, current, latest; *Ant.* 1. old, ancient, usual; 2. outmoded.

***Nice*** : *adj.* 1. pleasant, agreeable, pleasing; 2. kind, thoughtful, friendly, cordial; 3. accurate, precise, exact; 1.

unpleasant, disagreeable, nasty; 2. thoughtless, unkind; 3. careless, inexact.

***Nimble*** : *adj.* agile, spry, lively, quick; *Ant.* clumsy, awkward, oafish.

***Noble*** : *adj.* 1. honourable, honest, upright, virtuous, dignified; 2. aristocratic, titled, high-born, well-born, blue-blooded; *Ant.* 1. ignoble, base, dishonest; 2. lowbrow.

***Noise*** : *n.* tumult, uproar, clamour, din, racket, clatter, outcry; *Ant.* quiet, silence, peace.

***Noisy*** : *adj.* loud, clamorous, tumultuous; *Ant.* quiet, silent, peaceful.

***Normal*** : *adj.* 1. healthy, sound, whole; 2. regular, usual, customary, standard, routine; *Ant.* 2. odd, irregular, peculiar.

***Notable*** : *adj.* noteworthy, remarkable, noted, unusual, uncommon, conspicuous, distinctive, distinguished; *n.* celebrity, personality, star; *Ant. adj.* ordinary, usual, commonplace.

***Noted*** : *adj.* famous, well-known, clebrated, distinguished, farmed, notable; *Ant.* unknown, anonymous.

***Notice*** : *n.* 1. sign, poster, announcement, advertisement; 2. observation, attention, heed, note; 3. warning, advice, amonition; *vb.* observe, note, heed, regard, pay attention to; *Ant. vb.* ignore, disregard, overlook.

***Nourishment*** : *n.* sustenance, support, food, nutriment; *Ant.* deprivation, starvation.

***Numerous*** : *adj.* numberless, many, infinite; *Ant.* few, scanty.

# O

***Obedience*** : *n.* submission, docility; *Ant.* disobedience, rebelliousness.

***Obedient*** : *adj.* docile, yielding, respectful, obliging; *Ant.* rebellious, mutinous.

***Object*** : *vb.* protest, disapprove of, complain; *n.* 1. objective, goal, target, aim; 2. thing, article, tangible; *Ant. vb.* approve, agree, assent.

***Objection*** : *n.* protest, disapproval, doubt; *Ant.* agreement, assent, concurrence.

***Objective*** : *n.* aim, goal, purpose; *adj.* fair, just, imparital, unbiased; *Ant.* subjective, biased.

***Oblige*** : *vb.* 1. require, force, compel; 2. please, serve, favour; *Ant.* disoblige, free.

***Obscure*** : *adj.* 1. unknown, inconspicuous; 2. hidden, dim, unclear, indistinct; 3.dark, dim, murky, dusky, screen, veil, hide, conceal cover; *Ant. adj.* 1. famous, noted, distinguished; 2. clear, lucid, illumined. 3. bright.

***Observant*** : *adj.* watchful, alert, keen, vigilant, attentive; *Ant.* unobservant, inattentive.

***Observe*** : *vb.* 1. see, notice, look at, regard, witness, watch; 2. honour, keep, celebrate; 3. obey, follow, abide by; *Ant.* 1., 2. disregard.

***Obsolte*** : *adj.* old-fashioned, outdated, outmoded, antiquated; *Ant.* new, modern up-to-date, fashionable.

***Obstacle*** : *n.* block, stop, barrier, interference, obstruction; *Ant.* aid, support.

***Obstinate*** : *adj.* stubborn, opinionated, willful, pig-headed, inflexible; *Ant.* pliable, pliant, yielding.

***Obstruct*** : *vb.* block, stop, hinder, prevant, interfere; *Ant.* help, further.

***Obtain*** : *vb.* get, acquire, gain. procure. secure, attain; *Ant.* lose, forgo.

***Obvious*** : *adj.* clear, unquestionable, transparent, plain, unmistakable; *Ant.* subtle, hiden, unobtrusive.

***Occasional*** : *adj.* irregular, random, sporadic; *Ant.* regular, chronic, constant.

***Occasionally*** : *adj.* now and then, infrequently, seldom, irregularly; *Ant.* often, regularly.

***Odd*** : *adj.* strange, unusal, peculiar, queer, weird, extraordinary; *Ant.* ordinary, regular, unexceptional, straightforward.

***Offend*** : *vb.* 1. irritate, annoy, vex, anger, provoke, displease; 2. outrage, insult; *Ant.* 1. please, flatter, delight.

***Offensive*** : *adj.* 1. aggressive, attacking; 2. unpleasant, disagreeable, revolting, nauseous, sickening, nauseating, disgusting; *n.* attack; *Ant.adj.* 1. defensive, defending; 2. pleasing, pleasant, agreeable, attractive.

***Offer*** : *vb.* 1. present, tender, proffer,, submit; 2. volunteer; *n.* suggestion, proposal, presentation; *Ant. vb.* refuse, deny; *n.* refusal, denial.

***Offhand*** : *adj.* casual, informal, impromptu, unprepared; *Ant.* planned, considered, calculated, thought-out.

***Often*** : *adv.* frequently, oftentimes, regularly, usually; *Ant.* rarely, seldom, hardly.

***Old*** : *adj.* 1. aged, elderly; 2. used, worn, dilapidated, ragged, faded, broken-down; 3. former, ancient, olden, old-fashioned, antique; *Ant.* 1. young , youthful; 2. fresh, brand-new.

***Old-fashioned*** : *adj.* old, antiquated, outmoded, passe; *Ant.* new, up-to-date, fashionable, current, modern.

***Old-timer*** : *n.* oldster; veteran, master; *Ant.* newcomer.

***Omit*** : *vb.* 1. leave out, exclude, except, bar; 2. ignore, neglect, overlook; *Ant.* include.

***One-sided*** : *adj.* partial, biased, prejudiced, unfair; *Ant.* impartial, just.

***Onset*** : *n.* beginning, opening, start, commencement; *Ant.* end, conclusion, finale.

***Onward*** : *adv.* forward, ahead; *Ant.* backward.

***Open*** : *adj.* 1. unclosed, uncovered, accessible; 2. public, free, unrestricted, permitted; 3. free easy, candid: sincere, honest; 4. unoccupied, vacant, unfilled; *vb.* 1. start, begin, commence; 2. expand, spread, extend; *Ant. adj.* 1., 2. closed, shut, sealed; 3. private, secretive; 4. filled, taken; *vb.* 1. finish, end, stop; 2. close, clench.

***Open-handed*** : *adj.* generous, kind, charitable; *Ant.* tightfisted, stingy, mean .

***Open-hearted*** : *adj.* honest, frank, candid; *Ant.* devious, insincere.

***Open-minded*** : *adj.* fair, tolerant, liberal, just; *Ant.* bigoted, intolerant, prejudiced.

***Opponent*** : *n.* rival, competitor, contestant, antagonist; *Ant.* ally, colleague, team-mate.

***Oppose*** : *vb.* resist, battle, combat, withstand, thwart; *Ant.* support.

***Opposite*** : *adj.* 1. contrary, reverse, different; 2. facing; *Ant.* 1. same, like, similar.

***Opposition*** : *n.* 1. antagonism, resistance, defince, counteraction; 2. foe, enemy, contestant, adversary, antagonist, competition; *Ant.* 1. support, help , cooperation.

***Oppression*** : *n.* tyranny, injustice, cruelty, persecution; *Ant.* freedom, liberty.

***Optimism*** : *n.* hopefulness, confidence; *Ant.* pessimism, doubtfulness, cynicism.

***Oral*** : *adj.* spoken, uttered, verbal, said, vocal, voiced; *Ant.* written, printed.

***Orderly*** : *adj.* 1. neat, well-organised, regulated; 2. disciplined, well-organised, well-behaved; *Ant.* 1. messy, sloppy, undisciplined; 2. disorganised, haphazard.

***Ordinary*** : *adj.* 1. usual, common, customary, regular, normal; 2. average, medicore, everyday, undistinguished; *Ant.* 2. extraordinary unusual, special.

***Original*** : *adj.* 1. first, primary, beginning; 2. unique, new, fresh, novel, creative; *Ant.* 1. secondary; 2. outmoded, old-fashioned.

***Orignator*** : *n.* inventor, creator; discoverer; *Ant.* imitator, follower.

***Outrageous*** : *adj.* shocking, offensive, disgraceful, shameful, shameless, gross, contemptible; *Ant.* reasonable, sensible, prudent.

***Outset*** : *n.* beginning, start, commencement; *Ant.* end, climax.

***Outside*** :*n.* 1. exterior, surface, covering; 2. limit, bound; *Ant.* 1. inside, interior.

***Outsider*** : *n.* stranger, alien, foreigner; non-member; *Ant.* insider, intimate.

***Outstanding*** : *adj.* 1. important, well-known, famous, prominent, conspicuous, leading; 2. unpaid, overdue, due, owing; *Ant.* 1. ordinary, average.

***Overcast*** : *adj.* cloudy, clouded, dark; *Ant.* clear, sunny.

***Overcome*** : *vb.* 1. conquer, defeat, beat, subdue; 2. overpower, weaken, overwhelm; *Ant.* submit, yield.

***Overlook*** : *vb.* ignore, disregard, neglect, miss; *Ant.* notice.

***Overpower*** : *vb.* overwhelm, vanquish, overcome, conquer, subdue, defeat, beat; *Ant.* surrender.

# P

***Pacific*** : *adj.* peaceful, calm, peaceable, tranquil, quiet; gentle; *Ant.* turbulent, excited, riled.

***Pacify*** : *vb.* calm, quiet, tranquilise, smooth, lull; *Ant.* upset, excite, disturb.

***Pain*** : *n.* 1. distress, suffering, misery, ache, pang, torment, agony; 2. anguish, misery; *vb.* hurt, harm, distress, ache; *Ant. n.* 1. comfort, ease; 2. delight, joy.

***Painful*** : *adj.* agonizing, aching, inflamed, sore, throbbing; *Ant.* soothing.

***Painstaking*** : *adj.* careful, exacting, scrupulous; *Ant.* careless, slipshod.

***Pale*** : *adj.* 1. white, ashen, colourless, wan, pallid; 2. dim, faint, *vb.* whiten blanch; *Ant. adj.* 1. ruddy, flushed; 2. dark, bright.

***Panic*** : *n.* alarm, fear, dread, fright, terror; *vb.* terrify, frighten, alarm; *Ant. vb.* calm, soothe, tranquilise.

***Parallel*** : *n. adj.* similar, corresponding, like, resembling; *n.* 1. equal, match, counterpart; 2. similarity, likeness, resemblance, correspondence, resemble, correspond to, match, equal; *Ant. adj.* divergent.

**Pardon** : *n.* excuse, forgiveness; amnesty, acquittal, exoneration; *vb.* excuse, forgive, acquit, exonerate; *Ant. vb.* condemn, sentence.

**Part** : *n.* 1. portion, piece, section, fraction, fragment; 2. share, allotment, participation, interest; 3. role, character, *vb.* 1. divide, split, break up, disconnect; 2. depart, go, leave, quit; *Ant. n.* 1. whole, entirely.

**Partial** : *adj.* incomplete, unfinished, undone; 2. prejudiced, biased, one-sided, unfair unjust; *Ant.* 1. entire, complete, comprehensive.

**Partition** : *n.* 1. division, separation, distribution; 2. divider, screen separator, barrier, wall; *vb.* divide, separate, apportion; *Ant. n.* 1. joining, unification.

**Passable** : *adj.* acceptable, satisfactory, adequate, tolerable, fair; *Ant.* exceptional. extraordinary, superior.

**Passion** : *n.* 1. emotion, feeling, zeal, rapture, excitement; 2. love, desire, affection, liking, fondness, enthusiasm; *Ant.* indiffernce, apathy, coolness.

**Past** : *adj.* 1. gone, over, finished, done, done with; 2. former, preceding, prior; 3. recent, preceding; *n.* 1. antiquity, old times, the (good) old days, days of yore, yesterday; 2. experiences, former life, secret life; *Ant. adj.* 1. ahead. 2. present, future; *n.* 1. present; future.

**Patience** : *n.* 1. calmness, composure, passiveness, serenity, courage; 2. endurance, perseverance, persistence; *Ant.* 1. impatience, restlessness, impetuosity.

**Pause** : *n.* hestitation, rest, wait, interrution, delay, break, intermission, recess; *vb.* besitate, rest, wait, interrupt, break, delay, recess; *Ant. n.* continuity, perpetuity; *vb.* continue, perpetuate.

**Peace** : *n.* 1. quite, serenity, calm, peacefulness, tranquility; 2. pact, treaty, true, accord, armistice; *Ant.* agitation, upheaval, disturbance.

**Peaceable** : *adj.* peaceful, gentle, mild, calm, friendly, amiable pacific; *Ant.* hostile, warlike, aggressive .

**Peaceful** : *adj.* peaceable, quiet, calm, serene, tranquil; *Ant.* disrupted, agitated, riotous.

**Peak** : *n.* 1. top, summit, point, crest; 2. top, maximum, pinnacle; *Ant.* 2. base, bottom.

**Peculiar** : *adj.* 1. unusual, odd, strange, unfamiliar, uncommon, queer, outlandish, curious; 2. characteristic, special, unique, exclusive; *Ant.* 1. ordinary, regular, unspecial.

**Pedestrian** : *n.* walker, stroller; *adj.* ordinary, common, everyday, dull, commonplace; *Ant.* *adj.* unusual, fascinating, extraordinary, special.

**Penniless** : *adj.* poor, poverty-stricken, needy, destitute; *Ant.* rich, wealthy, well-off, prosperous.

**Perfect** : *adj.* 1. faultless, excellent, flawless, pure, ideal; 2. complete, finished, whole; 3. complete, utter, total; 4. exact, precise, sharp, correct; *vb.* complete, achieve, finish accomplish; *Ant.* *adj.* 1. imperfect, flawed, second-rate.

**Perhaps** : *adv.* may be, possibly, conceiveably; *Ant.* definitely absolutely.

**Peril** : *n.* danger, hazard, risk; *Ant.* security, safety.

**Perilous** : *adj.* dangerous, risky, hazardous, unsafe; *Ant.* safe, secure.

**Permanent** : *adj.* 1. enduring, lasting, stable, continuing, long-lived, persisting, persistent, perpetual, everlasting; 2. unchanging, unaltered, unchanged, constant, unvarying, invariable; *Ant.* passing, temporary, inconstant, fluctuating.

**Permit** : *vb.* allow, let, tolerate, suffer; *n.* license, permission, authorisation; *Ant.* *vb.* forbid, prohibit, disallow.

**Perpendicular** : *adj.* vertical, upright, standing; *Ant.* horizontal.

**Perpetual** : *adj.* unceasing, continuing, continuous, continual, everlasting, permanent, constant, eternal, ceaseless, undying; *Ant.* intermittent, inconstant, fluctuating.

***Persevere*** : *vb.* endure, persist, last, continue; *Ant.* lapse, desist, discontinue, stop.

***Persist*** : *vb.* persevere, continue, remain, endure; *Ant.* stop, desist.

***Personal*** : *adj.* 1. private, secret; 2. individual, special, particular; *Ant.* 1. public, general.

***Persuade*** : *vb.* 1. influence, induce, convince; 2. urge, coax, prompt; *Ant.* 1. dissuade, discourage.

***Persuasive*** : *adj.* convincing; influential, winning, alluring, compelling, stimulating; *Ant.* unconvincing; dubious.

***Petty*** : *adj.* 1. unimportant, trival, insignificant, paltry; 2. stingy, mean, miserly; *Ant.* 1. grand, vital, significant; 2. generous, big-hearted.

***Physical*** : *adj.* 1. bodily, corporeal, corporal; 2. real, material, natural; *Ant.* 1. mental, spiritual.

***Piecemeal*** : *adv.* partially, gradually; *Ant.* entire, whole, complete.

***Pious*** : *adj.* devout, religious, reverent; *Ant.* impious, irreligious, profane.

***Pity*** : *n.* sympathy, compassion, charity, mercy, tender heartedness, softheartedness; *vb.* feel for, sympathise (with), commiserate (with); *Ant. n.* cruelty, pitilessness, vindictiveness.

***Plain*** : *adj.* 1. simple, undecorated, unembellished, ordinary, unadorned; 2. homely, unattractive; 3. clear, understandable, unmistakable, obvious; 4. candid, blunt, outspoken, frank, open, honest, sincere; *n.* plateau, mesa, prairie, steppe, savanna, tundra; *Ant. adj.* 1. fancy, elaborate, ornamented; 2. pretty, beautiful, comely; 3. disguised, hidden, unclear.

***Pleasant*** : *adj.* 1. enjoyable, nice, agreeable, pleasurable, satisfying, satisfactory, adequate, acceptable; 2. affable, agreeable, charming, mild, amiable, friendly, personable, courteous; *Ant.* horrid, disagreeable, sour, nasty, difficult.

***Please*** : *vb.* 1. gratify, satisfy; 2. desire, choose, wish; *Ant.* 1. displease, annoy, vex.

***Pleasing*** : *adj.* pleasant, agreeable, charming, delightful, engaging; *Ant.* irritating, annoying.

***Pleasure*** : *n.* 1. delight, satisfaction, enjoyment, gladness, happiness, joy, well-being, gratification; 2. luxury, indulgence; *Ant.* 1. pain, discomfort, torment; 2. obligation, duty, responsibility.

***Plentiful*** : *adj.* abundant, bountiful, fullness, fruitful, copious; *Ant.* scarce, rare, scanty.

***Plenty*** : *n.* abundance, fullness, fruitfulness, bounty, plentifulness; *Ant.* need, want, scarcity.

***Plump*** : *adj.* chubby, fat, stout, portly, fleshy; *Ant.* slim, thin, skinny.

***Poise*** : *n.* 1. self-control, control, assurance, composure, dignity, carriage; 2. balance, steadiness, equilibrium; *vb.* balance, hesitate; *Ant. n.* 1. indelicacy, coarseness, boorishness, ineptitude; 2. awkwardness, instability, uncertainty.

***Polish*** : *vb.* 1. shine, brighten; 2. refine, finish; *n.* 1. gloss, shine, sheen, lustre, brightness; 2. refinement, finish, elegance; *Ant. vb.* 1. dull, tarnish.

***Polite*** : *adj.* courteous, thoughtful, mannerly, considerate, cordial, respectful; *Ant.* rude discourteous, uncivil.

***Pollute*** : *vb.* contaminate, dirty, befoul, taint; *Ant.* clean, purify, clarify.

***Poor*** : *adj.* 1. impoverished, poverty-stricken, needy, indigent, destitute, penniless, hard-up; 2. bad, sub-standard, faulty, inferior, worthless; 3. unfortunate, unlucky, doomed, luckless, unhappy, miserable, pitiful, pitiable; *Ant.* 1. rich, wealthy, well-heeled, prosperous, 2. good, excellent; 3. lucky, fortunate.

***Portly*** : *adj.* 1. dignified, grand, impressive, majestic; 2. corpulent, stout, fat, heavy, obese; *Ant.* 2. slim, thin, slender.

***Positive*** : *adj.* 1. clear, definite, sure, certain, direct, unmistakable;2. sure, certain, definite, obstinate; 3. practical, real; beneficial; *Ant.* 1., 2. unsure, dubious, mixed-up, confused. 3. negative, adverse.

***Potent*** : *adj.* powerful, strong, mighty, influential, convincing, effective; *Ant.* impotent, weak, powerless, feeble.

***Poverty*** : *n.* 1. need, want, indigence, destitution, distress, pennilessness; 2. scarcity, lack, scantiness, scarceness; *Ant.* 1 wealth, richness, comfort; 2. abundance, fruitfulness.

***Powerful*** : *adj.*strong, mighty, potent; 2. influential, effective, convincing; *Ant.* 1. weak, powerless; 2. ineffectual.

***Practical*** : *adj.* possible, workable, doable, achievable, attainable; *Ant.* impractical, visionary.

***Praise*** : *vb.* commend, laud, applaud, admire, celebrate; *n.* commendation, compliment, approval, kudos; *Ant. vb.* disapprove, condemn, criticise; *n.* criticism, negation.

***Practised*** : *adj.* skilled, adept, expert, able; *Ant.* inept.

***Precipitate*** : *adj.* sudden, swift, hasty, speedy; *Ant.* considered, gradual.

***Predominant*** : *adj.* prevalent, dominant, prevailing; *Ant.* secondary, accessory.

***Preoccupied*** : *adj.* distracted, absorbed, inattentive, meditative; *Ant.* alert, aware, conscious.

***Presence*** : *n.* 1. attendance; 2. nearness, vicinity, closeness; 3. bearing, personality, appearance; *Ant.* 1. absence.

***Preserve*** : *vb.* 1 keep, maintain, conserve, save; 2. can, conserve cure, salt, pickle; *Ant.* 1. squander, waste, use.

***Pretentious*** : *adj.* ostentatious, show-off, gaudy; *Ant.* humble, simple.

***Pretty*** : *adj.* attractive, comely, fair, lovely, beautful; *Ant.* plain, homely, ugly.

***Prevail*** : *vb.* 1. predominate; 2. succeed, win, triumph; *Ant.* 2. lose, yield.

***Prevalent*** : *adj.* common, prevailing, widespread, extensive; *Ant.* rare, infrequent.

***Prevent*** : *vb.* block, stop, thwart, halt, check, interrupt, obstruct, retard, hinder, slow, deter, inhibit; *Ant.* help, abet, allow.

***Previous*** : *adj.* prior, earlier, former; *Ant.* later, following, subsequent.

***Pride*** : *n.* 1. conceit, vanity, arrogance, self-importance, egotism, pretension; 2. self-respect, satisfaction; 3. enjoyment, fulfilment,, satisfaction; *Ant.* 1. humility, humbleness.

***Primary*** : *adj.* 1. chief, main, principal; 2. first, earliest, prime, original; 3. elementary, basic, fundamental, beginning; grammar; *Ant.* 1., 2. secondary.

***Primitive*** : *adj.* 1. prehistoric, primeval; 2. uncivilised, uncultured, unsophisticated, simple, rough, rude, brutish; *Ant.* 2. cultured, sophisticated, cultivated.

***Principal*** : *adj.* chief, main, leading, prime, first, essential, primary; *n.* chief, head, leader; headmaster, dean; *Ant. adj.* secondary, accessory.

***Prior*** : *adj.* earlier, sooner, preceding; *Ant.* subsequent, later.

***Private*** : *adj.* 1. personal, individual special, particular, confidential, hidden; *Ant.* 1. public, general.

***Prize*** : *n.* reward, award, premium, bounty, bonus; *vb.* value, esteem; estimate, rate; *Ant. vb.* undervalue, disregard.

***Proceed*** : *vb.* 1. move ahead *or* on, go on, progress, continue; 2. result, issue, spring, emanate: *Ant.* 1. withdraw, retreat.

***Productive*** : *adj.* fertile, fruitful, rich, creative; *Ant.* wasteful, useless.

***Profession*** : *n.* occupation, calling, vocation, employment; *Ant.* avocation, hobby, pastime.

***Profit*** : *n.* 1. gain, return, earnings; 2. advantage, benefit, gain, improvement; *vb.* gain, benefit, improve, better; *Ant. n.* 1. loss, debit; *vb.* lose.

***Profound*** : *adj.* deep, solemn, serious; wise, knowing, knowledgeable, intelligent, learned; *Ant.* shallow, superficial.

***Progress*** : *n.* advance, advancement, movement, improvement, development; *vb.* advance, improve, proceed, develop; *Ant. n.* regression. *vb.* regress, backslide.

***Prohibit*** : *vb.* 1. forbid, disallow, ban; 2. prevent, obstruct, stop, hinder; *Ant.* 1. allow, permit. 2. help, encourage.

***Probhition*** : *n.* ban, prevention, restriction, embargo; *Ant.* permission, allowance.

***Prominent*** : *adj.* 1. well-known, famous, noted, notable, noteworthy, important, eminent, distinguished, leading, celebrated; 2. noticeable, obvious, conspicuous; *Ant.* insignificant, unimportant.

***Prompt*** : *adj.* timely, punctual; *vb.* 1. urge, arouse, incite; 2. hint, suggest, propose, mention; *Ant. adj.* laggardly, tardy, late.

***Pronounced*** : *adj.* definite, clear, noticeable; *Ant.* indistinguishable, minor, unnoticeable.

***Prosper*** : *vb.* succeed, thrive, rise, flourish; *Ant.* wane, fail.

***Prosperous*** : *adj.* wealthy, well-off, rich, thriving, flourshing, well-to-do; *Ant.* poor, impoverished.

***Protest*** : *n.* objection, complaint, opposition, disagreement; *vb.* object, complain; *Ant. n.* approval, assent. *vb.* approve, assent.

***Prudence*** : *n.* 1. carefulness, care, caution, tact; 2. wisdom, judgement, foresight, commonsense; *Ant.* rashness, recklessness, foolishness.

***Prudent*** : *adj.* 1. wise, discreet, careful, sensible; 2. provident, reasonable; *Ant.* 1. rash, reckless, foolish, foolhardy.

***Public*** : *n.* society, people; *adj.* 1. common; governmental, municipal, civil, federal; 2. free; *Ant. adj.* private.

***Punctual*** : *adj.* prompt, timely, on time; *Ant.* tardy, late, laggardly.

***Punish*** : *vb.* discipline, chasten, castigate, reprove, lecture, scold; *Ant.* reward.

***Pure*** : *adj.* 1. unmixed, genuine, simple, undiluted; 2. spotless, untainted, clean, uncontaminated, unpolluted; 3. innocent, good, chaste, virtuous; *Ant.* 1. adulterated, mixed; 2. dirty, foul, tainted; 3. immoral, licentious.

# Q

***Quaint*** : *adj.* 1. strange, unusual, odd, curious, uncommon; 2. old-fashioned, antiquated, antique, picturesque; *Ant.* 1. common, commonplace, ordinary.

***Quarrelsome*** : *adj.* edgy, testy, irritable, peevish, snappish, diagreeable; *Ant.* even-tempered, genial.

***Queer*** : *adj.* odd, peculiar, unusual, extraordinary, uncommon; *Ant.* ordinary, conventional. usual.

***Question*** : *n.* 1. query, inquiry; 2. doubt, uncertainty; *vb.* 1. query, ask, inquire, interview; 2. doubt suspect *Ant. n.* 1. answer, solution; *vb.* 1. answer, reply, respond.

***Quick*** : *adj.* 1. rapid, swift, fast, speedy; 2. impatient, abrupt, hasty, curt; 3. prompt, ready, immediate; *Ant.* 1. slow, sluggish; 2. patient.

***Quiet*** : *adj.* 1. silent, still, soundless, mute; 2. tranquil, peaceful, calm, restful; *vb.* 1. silence, still, hushmute, soften; 2. calm, cool, relax, pacify, subdue, stillness, peace, peacefulness, calm, calmness; *Ant. adj.* 1. noisy, loud, boisterous; 2. perturbed, anxious; fitful.

# R

***Race*** : *n.* 1. contest, competition, run, meet, match; 2. stream, course; *vb.* 1. run, compete, contend; 2. hurry, run, speed, dash, hasten; *Ant. vb.* 2. dawdle, linger, dwell.

***Radiant*** : *adj.* bright, shining, beaming; brilliant; *Ant.* dim, lustreless, dark.

***Raise*** : *vb.* 1. lift, elevate, hoist; 2. rear, bring up, cultivate; 3. rouse, awaken, excite; 4. increase; enlarge; *n.* increase, rise; Ant *vb.* 1. lower; 4. decrease, lessen, reduce; *n.* decrease, reduction, cut.

***Random*** : *adj.* chance, haphazard, unplanned, unscheduled, irregular, casual; *Ant.* particular, specific, special.

***Rapid*** : *adj.* quick, swift, speedy, fast; *Ant.* slow, sluggish, halting.

***Rare*** : *adj.* 1. unusual, uncommon, scarce, infrequent; 2. excellent, fine, chic, matchless; 3. underdone, undercooked, red; *Ant.* 1. common, ordinary, usual, everyday.

***Rash*** : *adj.* thoughtless, hasty, hotheaded, foolhardy, reckless; *Ant.* considered, thoughtful, prudent.

***Rartional*** : *adj.* 1. sensible, reasonable; 2. sane, clearheaded, normal; *Ant.* 2. irrational, insane, crazy.

***Real*** : *adj.* true, actual, genuine, authentic; *Ant.* false, counterfeit, sham, bogus.

***Rear*** : *n.* back; rump, posterior, back; *Ant. n.* front.

***Reasonable*** : *adj.* 1. sensible, rational, logical; 2. moderate, bearable; *Ant.* 1. irrational, insane; 2. outrageous.

***Rebuke*** : *vb.* upbraid, chide, reproach, scold; *n.* reprimand, reproach, scolding; *Ant. vb. n.* praise.

***Receive*** : *vb.* 1. accept, get, acquire, come by, obtain; 2. entertain, greet, welcome; *Ant.* 1. give, offer.

***Recent*** : *adj.* late, up-to-date, new, novel; *Ant.* old, out-of-date, dated.

***Recollect*** : *vb.* remember, recall; *Ant.* forget.

***Recommend*** : *vb.* 1. commend, praise, approve; 2. advise, counsel, suggest; *Ant.* 1. disapprove, veto.

***Reduce*** : *vb.* 1. lessen, diminish, decrease; 2. lower, degrade, downgrade; *Ant.* 1. increase, enlarge, swell; 2. elevate, raise.

***Refined*** : *adj.* cultivated, polite, courteous, well-bred, civilised; *Ant.* rude, coarse, brutish.

***Refresh*** : *vb.* renew, exhilarate, invigorate; *Ant.* tire, exhaust.

***Regular*** : *adj.* 1. usual, customary, habitual, normal; 2. steady, uniform, even, systematic, orderly; *Ant.* irregular, odd, unusual.

***Reject*** : *vb.* 1. refuse, deny; renounce; 2. discard, expel, throw out or away; *Ant.* accept.

***Relax*** : *vb.* 1. loosen, slacken, let go; 2. repose, recline, unwind, rest; *Ant.* 1. tighten, increase, intensify.

***Reliable*** : *adj.* trustworthy, dependable; *Ant.* unreliable, erratic, eccentric.

***Religious*** : *adj.* 1. pious, devout, devoted, reverent, holy, faithful, godly; 2. strict, rigid, exacting, conscientious; *Ant.* 1. irreligious impious; 2. lax, slack, indifferent.

***Relish*** : *n.* 1. satisfaction, enjoyment, delight, appreciation, gusto; 2. condiment, enjoy, like, appreciate; *Ant. n.* 1. distaste, disfavour.

***Reluctant*** : *adj.* unwilling, hesitant, discinclined, loath; *Ant.* ready, eager.

***Remain*** : *vb.* stay, continue, linger; *Ant.* depart, leave, go.

***Remarkable*** : *adj.* unusual, special, extraordinary, noteworthy, uncommon; *Ant.* average, ordinary, commonplace.

***Remember*** : *vb.* 1. recall, recollect; 2. memorise, retain, know by heart, keep *or* bear in mind; *Ant.* forget.

***Remote*** : *adj.* 1. distant, far off *or* away; 2. slight, unlikely, inconsiderable; *Ant.* 1. near, nearby, close.

***Renown*** : *n.* fame, reputation, glory, distinction, prestige; *Ant.* anonymity, obscurity.

***Repel*** : *vb.* 1. repulse, check, rebuff; 2. refuse, reject, decline, discourage; 3. revolt, revulse, offend, nauseate; *Ant.* 3. attract, allure.

***Rescue*** : *vb.* save, set free, liberate, release, ransom, deliver; *n.* liberation, release, ransom, deliverance, recovery; *Ant. vb.* abandon.

***Reserve*** : *vb.* save, keep, hold, maintain; *Ant.* squander, waste.

***Resolute*** : *adj.* resolved, firm, determined, set, decided; *Ant.* wavering, irresolute, vacillating.

***Respect*** : *n.* 1. admiration, regard, honour, esteem, approval; 2. particular; regard, detail, point, feature; 3. reference, connection 4. concern, consideration; *vb.* honour, esteem, revere; *Ant. n.* 4. disrespect, disregard.

***Respectable*** : *adj.* 1. acceptable, proper, decent, respected;

2. fair, passable, presentable; *Ant.* 1. disreputable, unsavoury.

***Respectful*** : *adj.* polite, courteous, well-bred, well-behaved, well-mannered; *Ant.* rude, impertinent, flippant.

***Restful*** : *adj.* quiet, peaceful, calm, tranquil; *Ant.* disturbed, upsetting, tumultuous, agitated.

***Restless*** : *adj.* nervous, jumpy, fidgety, unquiet, restive; *Ant.* calm, tranquil, peaceful.

***Result*** : *n.* effect, outcome, consequence; *vb.* arise, happen, follow, issue; *Ant. n.* cause.

***Retain*** : *vb.* 1. hold, keep; 2. remember, recall; 3. hire, employ, engage; *Ant.* 1. free, release.

***Retard*** : *vb.* delay, hold back, slow, hinder, check, obstruct; *Ant.* advance, speed.

***Retarded*** : *adj.* backward, slow, behindhand, slow-witted, dull, stupid; *Ant.* advanced, quick.

***Retire*** : *vb.* 1. leave, part, withdraw, rotreat; 2. resign, leave; *Ant.* 1. advance, attack.

***Retiring*** : *adj.* shy, withdrawn, modest, reserved; *Ant.* bold, impudent, forceful.

***Retreat*** : *vb.* retire, leave, withdraw, depart; *n.* 1. departure, retirement, withdrawal; 2. shelter, hideaway, refuge; *Ant. vb.* advance.

***Reveal*** : *vb.* disclose, communicate, tell, divulge, publish, announce, publicise, broadcast; *Ant.* conceal, hide.

***Revere*** : *vb.* venerate, respect, admire; *Ant.* despise.

***Reverent*** : *adj.* respectful, honouring; *Ant.* disrespectful, impious.

***Revive*** : *vb.* 1. renew, refresh, reanimate, rejuvenate, reawaken; 2. recover, rewake; *Ant.* 2. tire, exhaust, enervate.

***Rich*** : *adj.* 1. wealthy, well-off, well-to-do, affluent; 2.

abundant, bountiful, plentiful, fruitful, fertile; *Ant.* 1. impoverished, poor; 2. scarce, unproductive, scanty.

***Ridicule*** : *vb.* mock, deride, taunt, tease: *n.* mockery, derision, burlesque, satire; *Ant. n.* respect, praise.

***Ridiculous*** : *adj.* nonesensical, farcical absurd, laughable, ludicrous., comic, preposterous; *Ant.* sensible, sound.

***Right*** : *adj.* 1. correct, fectual, accurate, true; 2. good, just, honest, upright, lawful, moral; 3. proper, suitable, apt, correct; *n.* 1. justice, virtue, morality, goodness, 2. title, claim, privilege; *adv.* 1. properly, correctly, legally, honourably, fairly; 2. directly, straight, straightaway; *Ant. adj.* 1. wrong, incorrect, fallacious.

***Rigid*** : *adj.* 1. stiff, unbending, unbendable, unyielding, inflexible; 2. severe, strict, stern, inflexible, harsh; *Ant.* flexible, lenient, soft, yielding.

***Ripe*** : *adj.* ready, mature, developed, grown aged; *Ant.* immature, ungrown.

***Risky*** : *adj.* dangerous, chancy, perilous, hazardous, unsafe; *Ant.* safe, secure.

***Romantic*** : *adj.* unpractical, extravagant, exaggerated, fantastic, wild; *Ant.* realistic, down-to-earth.

***Rotten*** : *adj.* 1. mouldy, decayed, spolied, decomposed, putrid, tainted, 2. corrupt, immoral dishonest, deceitful; *Ant.* 1. fresh.

***Rough*** : *adj.* 1. uneven, unpolished, irregular, bumpy; 2. coarse, impolite, unpolished, rude, crude, unrefined; 3. stormy, wild, violent, disorderly, turbulent; 4. uncomfortable, inconvenient; 5. unfinished, hasty, crude, vague, *Ant.* 1. smooth, sleek; 2. suave, sophisticated.

***Roundabout*** : *adj.* indirect, devious; *Ant.* direct, straightforward.

***Routine*** : *n.* way, method, system, habit, habitual, customary, usual; *Ant. adj.* uncommon, rare, unusual.

**_Rude_** : *adj.* impolite, crude, unmannerly, uncivil, ill-mannered, coarse, impudent, impertinent; *Ant.* courteous, polished, cultivated.

**_Rural_** : *adj.* rustic, pastoral, backwoods, country, farm, agricultural; *Ant.* urban, citified.

**_Rush_** : *vb.* run, hasten, speed, hurry, dash; *n.* haste, hurry; *Ant. vb.* linger, tarry.

# S

***Sacred*** : *adj.* holy, hallowed, divine, consecreated; *Ant.* blasphemous, profane.

***Sad*** : *adj.* 1. unhappy, downhearted, sorrowful, depressed, dejected, melancholy, glum, downcast, gloomy, cheerless; 2. saddening, discouraging, dismal, tragic; *Ant.* happy, joyous.

***Safe*** : *adj.* 1. protected, secure; 2. reliable trustworthy, dependable; *n.* vault, strongbox, safety, deposits box, *Ant. adj.* 1. dangerous.

***Sane*** : *adj.* rational, sound, normal, balanced, reasonable; *Ant.* insane, irrational, crazy.

***Sanitary*** : *adj.* clean, disinfected, hygienic, purified; *Ant.* dirty, unclean, fouled, soiled.

***Satisfactory*** : *adj.* sufficient, okay, all right, adequate; *Ant.* unsatisfactory, poor.

***Savage*** : *adj.* 1. wild, uncivilised, uncultivated, rough, rugged, crude, natural; 2. cruel, heartless, force, ferocious; *n.* aborigine, cannibal, native, barbarian; *Ant. adj.* 1. tame, cultivated.

***Scanty*** : *adj.* sparse, scarce, meagre, inadequate, insufficient,

*Ant.* plentiful, abundant.

**Scarce** : *adj.* rare, sparse, scanty, insufficient; *Ant.* common, usual.

**Scatter** : *vb.* spread, sprinkle, disperse; *Ant.* gather, collect, assemble.

**Secret** : *adj.* hidden, concealed, unknown; *n.* confidence; mystery; *Ant. adj.* open, public.

**Secure** : *adj.* 1. firm, tight, fast, fastened, stable, fixed; 2. safe, protected, defended; 3. assured, self-assured, confident, resolute; *vb.* 1. fasten, fix, tighten 2. obtain, procure, acquire; 3. protect, defend, guard; *Ant. adj.* 1. loose, free; 2. endangered.

**Seize** : *vb.* 1. grab, grasp, clutch; 2. capture, take; *Ant.* 1. release, loosen.

**Senior** : *adj.* older, elder, superior; *Ant.* junior, minor.

**Sensible** : *adj.* reasonable, rational, commonsensical; responsive, responsible; *Ant.* foolish.

**Serene** : *adj.* peaceful, quiet, calm, tranquil; *Ant.* agitated, turbulent, stormy.

**Serious** : *adj.* 1. grave, earnest, sober, solemn; 2. important, critical, *Ant.* 1. frivolous, jocular, light.

**Sever** : *vb.* cut, divide, split; *Ant.* join, connect.

**Severe** : *adj.* 1. cruel, strict, harsh, rigid, firm, unyielding; 2. difficult, harsh, unpleasant; 3. violent, dangerous; *Ant.* 1. lenient, easy going. 2. mild.

**Shameless** : *adj.* unashamed, unembarrassed, bold, brazen, insolent, impudent; *Ant.* modest, demure.

**Sharp** : *adj.* keen, acute, cutting, fine; *Ant.* blunt, dull.

**Shiny** : *adj.* glossy, polished, bright, glistening; *Ant.* dull, lustreless.

**Shipshape** : *adj.* neat, clean, Bristol-fashion; *Ant.* messy, sloppy.

***Short*** : *adj.* 1. brief, concise, abbreviated, condensed, curtailed, terse, abridged; 2. slight, little, undersized, scanty; *Ant.* 1. long, lengthy; 2. tall.

***Shorten*** : *vb.* 1. cut, curtail, abbreviate, abridge; 2. take in, lessen, reduce; *Ant.* lengthen.

***Shrill*** : *adj.* sharp, piercing; *Ant.* muted, muffled.

***Shrink*** : *vb.* 1. contract, diminish, dwindle, shrivel; 2. recoil, withraw, flinch, retreat; *Ant.* 1. swell.

***Shut*** : *vb.* close; lock, seal; *Ant.* open.

***Shy*** : *adj.* timid, bashful; *Ant.* bold, self-confident, brazen.

***Significant*** : *adj.* important, meaningful, vital, crucial, critical; *Ant.* unimportant, insignificant, trivial.

***Silence*** : *n.* 1. quiet, stillness, noselessness, soundlessness, hush 2. muteness, speechlessness, *Ant.* 1. noisiness, clamour, racket.

***Silent*** : *adj.* 1. quiet, noiseless, soundless, still, hushed; 2. mute, speechless, uncommunicative; *Ant.* 1. noisy, clamorous; 2. talkative, communicative.

***Similar*** : *adj.* like, resembling, alike; *Ant.* different, dissimilar.

***Simple*** : *adj.* 1. uncomplicated; 2. clear, understandable, plain; 3. easy; *Ant.* 1. complicated, complex; 2. difficult, abstruse; 3. demanding.

***Skillful*** : *adj.* skilled, accomplished, expert, adept, proficient; *Ant.* inept, clumsy, awkward.

***Skinny*** : *adj.* thin, scrawny, gaunt, raw-boned; *Ant.* heavy, hefty, fat.

***Slack*** : *adj.* 1. loose, lax, limp; 2. lazy; 3. slow, inactive, sluggish; *Ant.* 1. taut, stiff, rigid; 3. active busy.

***Slender*** : *adj.* slim, trim, slight, thin; *Ant.* heavy, fat, overweight.

***Slight*** : *adj.* 1. small, sparse, scanty, sparse; 2. insignificant, unimportant, trivial; *vb.* ignore, disregard, snub, scorn; *Ant. adj.* 1. large, enormous, huge. 2. major, significant. *vb.* flatter, compliment.

***Slow*** : *adj.* 1. unhurried, gradual, leisurely; 2. late, delayed, behindhand; 3. dull, boring, tedious; *vb.* retard, hinder, obstruct, slacken; *Ant.* 1. fast, quick; 2. fast, ahead.

***Small*** : *adj.* 1. little, tiny, miniature; 2. unimportant, insignificant, minor, trivial; *Ant.* 1. large, big, enormous.

***Smart*** : *adj.* clever, intelligent, bright; *vb.* sting, hurt, burn; *Ant. adj.* stupid, slow, dumb.

***Smile*** : *n.* grin; *vb.* grin, beam; *Ant. n. vb.* scowl, frown.

***Smooth*** : *adj.* even, level, flat, unwrinkled; *vb.* level, even, flatten, iron; *Ant. adj.* rough, uneven.

***Sobre*** : *adj.* 1. clear-headed, moderate; 2. serious, solemn, grave; *Ant.* 1. drunk, inebriated, fuddled. 2. frivolous.

***Soft*** : *adj.* flexible, pliable, pliant; elastic; 2. smooth, velvety, satiny; 3. quiet, low, gentle; *Ant.* 1. hard, rigid.

***Solemn*** : *adj.* 1. serious, sobre, grave, 2. formal, serious dignified; *Ant.* 1. cheerful, happy, gay.

***Solid*** : *adj.* 1. firm, compact, hard, dense; 2. three-dimensional; 3. unmixed, plain; *Ant.* 1. loose.

***Sombre*** : *adj.* 1. serious, sobre, grave, gloomy, dismal; 2. dismal, mournful, sad, mealancholy; *Ant.* 1. happy, cheerful, gay.

***Sometimes*** : *adv.* occasionally, now and then; *Ant.* always, invariably.

***Soothe*** : *vb.* calm, pacify, comfort, quite; *Ant.* disquiet, upset, unnerve.

***Sorry*** : *adj.* regretful, apologetic; *Ant.* happy, glad.

***Sour*** : *adj.* 1. acid, tart; 2. bad-tempered, unpleasant, touchy, cross, cranky; *Ant.* 1. sweet. 2. good-natured, sunny, benevolent.

**Spacious** : *adj.* roomy, large; *Ant.* cramped, small, narrow, confined.

**Special** : *adj.* 1. exceptional, unusual, extraordinary, different, particular; 2. distinct, certain, unusual; *Ant.* 1. average, ordinary.

**Specific** : *adj.* definite, particular, distinct, precise; *Ant.* general, nonspecific.

**Spectator** : *n.* watcher, viewer, observer, onlooker; *Ant.* participant.

**Spend** : *vb.* 1. pay, expend, disburse; 2. use up, consume; *Ant.* 1. save, hoard.

**Spineless** : *adj.* weak, feeble, limp; cowardly; *Ant.* strong, brave, courageous.

**Spirited** : *adj.* animated, excited, active, lively, energetic, vigorous; *Ant.* lazy, indolent, sleepy.

**Spontaneous** : *adj.* natural, voluntary, unconscious, unplanned; *Ant.* studied, cautious.

**Spry** : *adj.* lively, nimble, quick, alert, agile, energetic; *Ant.* inactive, lethargic.

**Stable** : *adj.* steady, firm, sturdy, steadfast, solid; *Ant.* unstable, shaky.

**Stale** : *adj.* 1. old, spoiled, dry, inedible; 2. uninteresting, flat, dull, trite, *Ant.* 1. fresh, new.

**Stand** : *vb.* 1. rise, arise, stand up; 2. remain , stay; 3. tolerate, endure, abide, bear; *n.* 1. position, attitude, opinion; 2. table, platform; *Ant. vb.* 1. lie, recline, repose.

**Stately** : *adj.* grand, dignified, imposing, elegant, impressive, majestic, magnificent, *Ant.* mean, base, squalid.

**Stay** : *vb.* 1. remain, rest, tarry, linger; 2. remain, continue; 3. delay, check, hinder, halt, hold; *n.* 1. stop, hindrance, check, halt, delay, 2. brace support, rope, line, shroud; *Ant. vb.* 1. go, leave depart.

***Stealthy*** : *adj.* secret, sly, furtive; *Ant.* open, direct, obvious.

***Steep*** : *adj.* sheer, perpendicular; *Ant.* gradual.

***Stern*** : *adj.* strict, severe, harsh, hard, rigid, unyielding; *Ant.* lenient, forgiving.

***Stiff*** : *adj.* 1. rigid, unbendable, inflexible, firm, solid, hard; 2. cool, cold, unfriendly; 3. severe, hash, strong; *Ant.* 1. limp lax; 2. warm hospitable; 3. lenient.

***Stingy*** : *adj.* miserly, mean, tightfisted, penny-pinching, cheap; selfish; *Ant.* generous, openhanded, giving.

***Stout*** : *adj.* 1. fat, obese, overweight, plump, heavy, portly; 2. strong, sturdy; *Ant.* 1. slim, thin, skinny, lean; 2. filmsy.

***Straight*** : *adj.* 1. direct, uncurving; 2. honest, upright, honourable, moral; 3. orderly correct; *adv. Ant. adj.* 1. crocked, twisted.

***Stranger*** : *n.* foreigner, alien, outsider; outlander; *Ant.* friend, acquaintance.

***Strength*** : *n.* 1. power, vigour, might; 2. durability, soundness; *Ant.* 1. weakness, frailty.

***Stretch*** : *vb.* 1. extend, elongate, lengthen; 2. expand; spread extend; *Ant.* contract, shrink.

***Strict*** : *adj.* stern; unbending, inflexible, stiff, harsh; *Ant.* lenient easygoing.

***Strife*** : *n.* conflict, disagreement, discord, difference, quarrel, unrest; *Ant.* peace, tranquility, concord.

***Strong*** : *adj.* 1. powerful, mighty, brawny, muscular; 2. solid, resistant, unbreakable; 3. sharp, spicy, hot aromatic; *Ant.* 1. feeble, weak; 2. frangile; 3. bland, tasteless.

***Stupid*** : *adj.* dumb, dull, half-witted, thimble-witted, witless, wimple-minded, idiotic; *Ant.* intelligent, smart, bright, quick.

***Sturdy*** : *adj.* rugged, strong, well-built, stout; *Ant.* frail, flimsy.

***Submerge*** : *vb.* dip, sink, submerse; *Ant.* rise, surface.

***Submit*** : *vb.* 1. yield, surrender; 2. offer, tender; *Ant.* 1. resist, fight.

***Subordinate*** : *adj.* inferior, lower; *n.* worker, assistant, inferior; *vb.* lower, demean, reduce; *Ant. adj. n.* superior.

***Subsequent*** : *adj.* following , later, succeding; *Ant.* previous, preceeding

***Subside*** : *vb.* sink, lower, diminish; *Ant.* erupt, arise.

***Substantial*** : *adj.* 1. considerable, large, sizeable; 2. real, actual, tangible; 3. wealthy, influential;*Ant.* 1. trivial, unimportant.

***Subtle*** : *adj.* indirect; suggestive; *Ant.* obvious, overt.

***Subtract*** : *vb.* reduce, diminish, deduct, lessen; *Ant.* add.

***Succeed*** : *vb.* 1. thrive, prosper, flourish; 2. follow, ensue; replace; *Ant.* 1. fail, flop; 2. precede.

***Success*** : *n.* prosperity, advance, luck; *Ant.* failure.

***Suffix*** : *n.* ending; *Ant.* prefix.

***Suitable*** : *adj.* fitting, apt, becoming, proper; *Ant.* inappropirate, unsuitable.

***Sullen*** : *adj.* 1. silent, moody, bitter, sulky; 2. dismal, sad, gloomy, sombre; *Ant.* 1. cheerful, cheery, jovial.

***Summit*** : *n.* top, peak, crown; *Ant.* base, bottom.

***Summon*** : *vb.* call, invoke, convoke, invite; *Ant.* dismiss.

***Superior*** : *adj.* better, greater, finer; *n.* boss, employer, supervisor; *Ant. adj.*, *n.* inferior.

***Surge*** : *vb.* swell, heave, grow; *Ant.* ebb, wane, diminish.

***Surrender*** : *vb.* yield, submit, give up; *Ant.* resist.

***Survive*** : *vb.* remain, perist, live, continue; *Ant.* fail, die. succumb.

***Suspect*** : doubt. mistrust, distrust, disbelieve; 2. suppose, presume, assume; *n.* defendant; suspicious, suspected, questionable, doubtful; *Ant. vb.* 1. know, believe, trust.

***Sweet*** : *adj.* 1. sugary, honeyed; 2. fresh, clean, pure, unsalted; 3. pleasant, melodious, tuneful, musical, harmonious, mellow; 4. charming, agreeable, pleasant, attractive; *Ant.* 1. sour, bitter; 3. discordant, harsh; 4. irritable, nasty, irascible.

***Swell*** : *vb.* grow, increase, enlarge, expand; *Ant.* shrink, diminish.

***Swift*** : *adj.* fast, quick, rapid, speedy, fleet; *Ant.* slow, sluggish, laggardly.

***Sympathetic*** : *adj.* compassionate, considerate, tender, kind; *Ant.* unsympathetic, intolerant, indifferent.

***Systematic*** : *adj.* organised, orderly, regular, methodical; *Ant.* random, irregular.

# T

***Tactful*** : *adj.* diplomatic, considerate, sensitive, skillful; *Ant.* tactless, unfeeling.

***Tall*** : *adj.* high, big; *Ant.* short, low

***Tame*** : *adj.* 1. domesticated, docile, mild, broken; 2. dull uninteresting, unexciting flat, empty, boring; *vb.* domesticate, break; *Ant. adj.* 1 wild.

***Tardy*** : *adj.* late, overdue, behindhand; *Ant.* prompt, punctual.

***Tedious*** : *adj.* tiring, tiresome, dull, boring, wearisome; *Ant.* interesting, engaging, exciting.

***Temperamental*** : *adj.* moody, irritable, touch, testy, sensitive; *Ant.* serene, unruffled.

***Temporary*** : *adj.* passing, short-lived, short, fleeting, momentary; *Ant.* permanent, everlasting, fixed.

***Tender*** : *adj.* 1. delicate, soft, fragile; 2. loving, gentle, affectionate, sympathetic; 3. sensitive, sore, painful; *Ant.* 1. tough, chewy; 2. unfeeling, cruel.

***Tenderhearted*** : *adj.* sympathetic, softhearted, kind, merciful; *Ant.* hardhearted, cruel.

***Tense*** : *adj.* stretched, strained, tight, excited, nervous; *Ant.* relaxed, lax.

***Terminate*** : *vb.* end, stop, cease, close, finish, conclude; *Ant.* begin, commence, start.

***Thaw*** : *vb.* melt, liquelfy, dissolve; *Ant.* freeze, solidify.

***Thick*** : *adj.* 1. dense, solid; 2. heavy, compact, syrupy, viscous; *Ant.* 1. thin, slim; 3. watery.

***Thorough*** : *adj.* complete, careful, thoroughgoing, completed; *Ant.* careless, haphazard, slapdash.

***Thoroughfare*** : *n.* street, highway, avenue, boulevard, parkway; *Ant.* alley, byway

***Thoughful*** : *adj.* 1. kind, considerate, attentive, courteous, friendly; 2. absorbed, pensive, reflective; *Ant.* 1. thoughtless.

***Thrifty*** : *adj.* frugal, sparing, parsimonious, economical, saving; *Ant.* spendthrift, prodigal.

***Thrive*** : *vb.* prosper, succeed, grow, flourish; *Ant.* languish expire, die.

***Tight*** : *adj.* 1. firm, taut, secure, strong, fast, fixed; 2. sealed, airtight, watertight locked, fastened, 3. tipsy, high, drunk, intoxicated, inebriated; 4. stingy, miserly, niggardly; *Ant.* 1. loose, slack;. 3. sober.

***Timid*** : *adj.* shy, bashful, retiring, coy, fainthearted, diffident, fearful; *Ant.* bold, forward, self-confident.

***Tiny*** : *adj.* small, wee, little, miniature; *Ant.* large, huge, enormous.

***Tire*** : *vb.* 1. weary, weaken, exhaust; 2. weary, weaken, fatigue, exhaust; *Ant.* exhilarate.

***Toil*** : *vb.* work, labour, slave, sweat; *n.* work, labour, drudgery, effort, exertion; *Ant. vb.* relax, loll.

***Tolerant*** : *adj.* considerate, patient, liberal, impartial; *Ant.* intolerant, biased, bigoted, prejudiced.

***Top*** : *n.* 1. peak, summit, tip, pinnacle; 2. cap, cover, lid; *vb.* excel, surpass, outdo, exceed, beat, better; *Ant. n.* 1. bottom, base.

***Touchy*** : *adj.* sensitive, jumpy, nervous, testy, short-tempered, irritable, *Ant.* calm, collected.

***Tough*** : *adj.* 1. strong, hard; 2. leathery, inedible, sinewy; *Ant.* 1. weak, vulnerable; 2. tender.

***Tragedy*** : *n.* misfortune, unhappiness misery; *Ant.* comedy.

***Tragic*** : *adj.* sad, unfortunate, miserable, depressing, mournful mealancholy; *Ant.* comic.

***Tranquil*** : *adj.* peaceful, calm, undisturbed, quiet; *Ant.* disturbed, upset, agitated.

***Transparent*** : *adj.* 1. clear, limpid; 2. clear, obvious evident, plain; *Ant.* 1. opaque.

***Treachery*** : *n.* betrayal, disloyalty, treason; *Ant.* loyalty, steadfastness.

***Triumph*** : *n.* conquest, victory, success; *vb.* win, prevail, succeed; *Ant. n.* defeat, failure.

***Trusted*** : *adj.* reliable, trustworthy, dependable, true, loyal, devoted, staunch; *Ant.* untrustworthy.

***Tumult*** : *n.* to-do, ado, confusion, disturbance, commotion, disorder, uproar; *Ant.* peacefulness, tranquility.

***Typical*** : *adj.* representative. characteristic; *Ant.* atypical, odd.

# U

***Unassuming*** : *adj.* modest, humble, retiring; *Ant.* vain, showy, pompous, arrogant.

***Uncertain*** : *adj.* unsure, doubtful, dubious, questionable, indefinite, vague; *Ant.* certain, positive, unmistakable.

***Uncommon*** : *adj.* rare, unusual scarce, odd, peculiar, strange, queer, remarkable, exceptional; *Ant.* usual, ordinary.

***Uncouth*** : *adj.* vulgar, rude, ill-mannered, discourteous, impolite; *Ant.* civilised, cultivated, cultured.

***Under*** : *prep.* 1. beneath, below, underneath; 2. following, below, in accordance with; *Ant.* 1. above, over.

***Underhand*** : *adj.* secret, sly, crafty, sneaky, stealthy, secretive; *Ant.* open, honest, direct.

***Unexpected*** : *adj.* surprising, sudden, abrupt, startling, unforeseen; *Ant.* expected, predicted, anticipated.

***Unhappy*** : *adj.* miserable, sad, mealancholy, wretched, distressed; *Ant.* happy, joyful, joyous.

***Unhealthy*** : *adj.* sick, sickly, infirm, diseased; *Ant.* healthy, well, hale.

***Unique*** : *adj.* single, sole, solitary, incomparable; *Ant.* common, ordinary, commonplace.

***Unite*** : *vb.* join, combine, connect, link, associate; *Ant.* divide, separate, sever.

***Universal*** : *adj.* general, prevailing, prevalent, common; *Ant.* local, regional.

***Unruly*** : *adj.* disorganised, unmanageable, disobedient, disorderly; *Ant.* orderly.

***Urge*** : *vb.* 1. force, push, drive, press, prod; 2. plead, persuade, beg, implore; 3. advise, recommend; *n.* impulse; *Ant. vb.* dissuade, discourage.

# V

***Vacant*** : *adj.* 1. unoccupied, empty, uninhabited, untenanted; 2. thoughless, vapid, vacuous, stupid; *Ant.* 1. full, filled, occupied. 2. bright, alert, intelligent.

***Vague*** : *adj.* uncertain, indefinite, unsure, obscure; *Ant.* specific, unequivocal.

***Vain*** : *adj.* 1. useless, worthless, idle, trivial, unfruitful, unsuccessful; 2. proud, conceited, self-important, arrogant; *Ant.* 2. humble.

***Valuable*** : *adj.* 1. important, worthy; 2. costly, high priced; *Ant.* 2. worthless.

***Vanish*** : *vb.* disappear, evaporate, dissolve; *Ant.* appear.

***Variable*** : *adj.* changeable, shifting, unsteady; *Ant.* constant, unwavering.

***Verbal*** : *adj.* spoken, oral; unwritten; *Ant.* written printed.

***Vertical*** : *adj.* upright, perpendicular, erect; *Ant.* horizontal.

***Veto*** : *n.* denial, refusal; *vb.* deny, refuse, negate, prohibit, forbid; *Ant. n.* approval, *vb.* approve.

***Victor*** : *n.* winner, champion, counquerer; *Ant.* loser, vanquished.

***Victory*** : *n.* conquest, success, triumph; *Ant.* defeat.

***Vigilant*** : *adj.* watchful, alert, attentive, observant, *Ant.* negligent, careless.

***Violent*** : *adj.* powerful, forceful, strong forcible; 2. furious, angry, savage, fierce, passionate; *Ant.* 2. gentle.

***Virtue*** : *n.* 1. goodness, morality, righteousness, honour 2. merit, quality, advantage; *Ant.* vice.

***Voluntary*** : *adj.* spontaneous, optional, free; *Ant.* compulsory, required, forced.

# W

***Wake*** : *vb.* 1. rouse, arouse, awaken, waken; 2. activate, stimulate; *Ant.* 1. sleep, doze.

***Waken*** : *vb.* See *wake*.

***War*** : *n.* hostilities, combat, battle; *vb.* battle, fight; *Ant.* peace.

***Warn*** : *adj.* 1. heated, temperate, tepid, lukewarm; 2. eager, enthusiastic, sympathetic; *vb.* heat; *Ant. adj.* 1. cool, cold, brisk; 2. indifferent; cool.

***Weak*** : *adj.* 1. feeble, frail, fragile, delicate; 2. diluted, watery; irresolute, unsteady, wavering; *Ant.* 1. strong, powerful.

***Wealthy*** : *adj.* rich, well-to-do, prosperous, affluent; *Ant.* poor, destitute, improverished, poverty-stricken.

***Wet*** : *adj.* soaked, drenched, moist, damp, dank; *vb.* soak, drench, moisten, dampen; *Ant. adj.* dry, arid, parched.

***Whole*** : *adj.* 1. entire, complete, undivided, uncut, total; 2. unbroken, undamaged, entire, intact; *Ant.* 1. part, partial.

***Wide*** : *adj.* broad, extensive; *Ant.* narrow, thin.

**Wild** : *adj.* 1. uncontrolled, unrestrained, unruly; 2. primitive, savage; 3. silly, impetuous, crazy, foolish; 4. untamed, ferocious, undomesticated; *Ant.* 1. restrained; 4. tame.

**Win** : *vb.* 1. succeed, gain, 2. obtain, gain acquire, get, earn; *Ant.* lose, forfeit.

**Wise** : *adj.* 1. intelligent, sensible, reasonable, sage, judicious 2. learned, knowledgeable, sage; smart; *Ant.* 1. foolish, foolhardy.

**Withdraw** : *vb.* remove, retract, recall; 2. retreat, retire, depart, go, secede; *Ant.* 1. place, enter.

**Wrong** : *adj.* 1. incorrect, inaccurate, false; 2. bad, naughty, improper. 3. improper, inappropriate, unsuitable, 4. awry, out of order, amiss; *adv.* improperly, incorrectly, *n.* 1. evil, wickedness, sin; 2. impropriety, incorrectness; *vb.* injure, harm, abuse, hurt; *Ant. adj.* 1. right, correct, accurate; 2. good, proper.

# Y

***Young*** : *adj.* 1. youthful, immature; 2. undeveloped, underdeveloped; *Ant.* 1. old, mature, grown.

***Youngster*** : *n.* lad, youth, stripling, child; *Ant.* adult, grownup.

# Z

***Zealous*** : *adj.* ardent, eager, enthusiastic; *Ant.* unenthusiastic.

# HOMONYMS

Words pronounced the same but differing in spelling and in meaning.

1. ***Air***, that which we breathe.
   ***Ere***, before.
   ***E'er***, ever.
   ***Heir***, one that is to inherit.
2. ***Aloud***, audibly.
   ***Allowed***, permitted.
3. ***Altar***, a place for worship.
   ***Alter***, to change.
4. ***Arc***, part of a circle.
   ***Ark***, as Noah's ark; a chest
5. ***Ascent***, going up; an upward slope.
6. ***Assent***, to agree to.
7. ***Ate***, past tense of eat.
   ***Eight***, twice four.
8. ***Aught***, anything
   ***Ought***, is (are) bound in duty.
9. ***Bad***, ill or wicked.
10. ***Bade***, past tense of bid.
    ***Bale***, a bundle.
    ***Bail***, surety for some one; a handle.
11. ***Ball***, a sphere; a dance.
    ***Bawl***, to shout; to cry out.
12. ***Band***, that which binds; a narrow strip.
    ***Banned***, forbidden.
13. ***Bard***, a poet.
    ***Barred***, hindered; shut out.

14. ***Bare***, naked.
***Bear***, to carry; a wild beast.
15. ***Base***, the lowest part; mean.
***Bass***, the lowest in harmonised music.
16. ***Beech***, a kind of tree.
***Beach***, shore.
17. ***Beer***, a drink.
***Bier***, anything on which the dead are carried to burial.
18. ***Beet***, a vegetable.
***Beat***, to strike.
19. ***Bell***, hollow metal body that rings of tolls.
***Belle***, a beautiful or admired young woman.
20. ***Berry***, a small fruit.
***Bury***, to inter; to conceal.
21. ***Birth***, being born; descent.
***Berth***, a sleeping place.
22. ***Bold,***, daring, courageous.
***Bowled***, rolled, as in a game of bowling.
23. ***Bole***, the trunk of a tree.
***Boll***, seed vessel of cotton plant.
***Bowl***, a circular vessel.
24. ***Bow***, a weapon for shooting arrows; a kind of knot.
***Beaw***, a man of dress: a lover.
25. ***Brake***, a thicket.
***Break*** , to split.
26. ***Bread***, baked flour.
***Bred***, reared.
27. ***Breech***, the lower or hinder part of a thing.
***Breach***, a gap or opening.
28. ***Brews***, ferments; plots.
***Bruise***, to crush; a contusion.
29. ***Broach***, a spit; to pierce.
***Brooch***, an ornament for the breast.
30. ***Brows***, the forehead.
***Browse***, to cut the tender leaves of shrubs, as sheep browse .
31. ***Burrow***, hole in ground made by an animal.
***Borough***, a corporate town.
***Burro***, a donkey.
32. ***By*** , a preposition and a prefix.
***Buy***, to purchase.
***Bye***, as in good-bye; a goal.
***Bli-***, two as in biweekly.
33. ***Call***, cry out: a visit.
***Caul***, a membrane.
34. ***Canon***, a law; a rule.
***Cannon***, a large gun.
35. ***Canvas***, a coarse cloth.
***Canvass***, to solicit.
36. ***Cast***, to throw. a form.
***Caste***, a tribe: a class.
37. ***Cede***, to give up.
***Seed***, the embryo of a future plant.

38. ***Ceiling***, cover of a room.
***Sealing***, tight closing, as with wax.
39. ***Cell***, a small cavity; a room.
***Sell***, to exchange for a price.
40. ***Cellar***, an excavation in the ground.
***Celler***, one who sells.
41. ***Cent***, a hundred.
***Sent***, past tense of send.
***Scent***, perume; to smell.
42. ***Cereal***, pertaining to grain; food made of grain.
***Serial***, pertaining to successive parts as in a series.
***Cession***, a giving up.
***Session***, a sitting a meeting.
43. ***Chews***, grinds with the teeth.
44. ***Choose***, to select.
***Choir***, a company of singers.
45. ***Quire***, a set of sheets of paper.
46. ***Cite***, to summon; to quote.
***Site***, place position.
***Sight***, the power of seeing a look.
47. ***Clause***, part of a sentence.
***Claws***, sharp nails or toes of animal or bird.
48. ***Clime***, a region; a country.
***Climb***, to mount; to ascend.
***Core***, an innermost part; a center.
49. ***Corps***, an organised company, as of soldiers.
50. ***Course***, a place for running; career.
***Coarse***, not fine.
***Coward***, one wanting in courage.
***Cowered***, crouched through fear.
51. ***Creek***, a small stream.
***Creak***, to make a harsh, grating noise.
52. ***Crews***, bodies of seamen for ships.
***Cruise***, to sail from place to place on the ocean.
***Cruse***, a small cup; a small bottle.
53. ***Currents***, streams.
***Currants***, small fruit.
54. ***Dew***, moisture condensed and deposited from the air.
***Due***, owing.
55. ***Discreet***, prudent; cautious.
***Discrete***, distinct; disjoined.
56. ***Doe***, female of deer.
***Do***, a musical second name.
***Dough***, unbaked bread.
57. ***Done***, performed.

**Dun**, a color; to demand payment of debt.

58. ***Dying***, ceasing to live.
***Dyeing***, shading or coloring.

59. ***Faint***, very fatgued; to swoon.
***Feint***, a pretence.

60. ***Fane***, a temple.
***Fain***, anxious desirous.
***Feign***, to pretend.

61. ***Fare***, money paid for a journey; food.
***Fair***, beautiful, right a market.

62. ***Faun***, a sylvan deity.
***Fawn***, a young deer; to flatter meanly.

63. ***Find***, to discover.
***Fined***, subject to a money penalty.

64. ***Flour,***, fine part of meal.
***Flower***, a blossom of a plant.

65. ***Fore***, in front.
***Four***, a number.

66. ***Forth***, forward out.
***Fourth***, the ordinal of four.

67. ***Freeze***, to congeal.
***Frieze***, a coarse wollen fabric; an ornamented band on a wall.

68. ***Gate***, entrance; a door.
***Gait***, one's way of walking.

69. ***C d***, to overlay and adorn with gold.
***Guild***, a society or corporation.

70. ***Gilt***, overlaid with good.
***Guilt***, responsibility for crime.

71. ***Great***, large.
***Grate***, a fireplace; to rub against.

72. ***Groan***, deep sound of pain or sorrow.
***Grown***, mature, fully developed.

73. ***Guessed***, estimated at random.
***Guest***, one who is entertained.

74. ***Hair***, as of the head.
***Hare***, an animal.

75. ***Hall***, a large room.
***Haul***, to drag; to pull.

76. ***Heel***, the hind part of the foot.
***Heal***, to cure; to grow sound.
***He'll***, a contraction for "he will".

77. ***Herd***, a collection of cattle.
***Heard***, past tense of hear.

78. ***Hoard***, to lay up in secret.
***Horde***, a wandering tribe; a savage band.

79. ***Hoes***, uses a hoe.
***Hose***, stockings, socks.
***Hose***, rubber pipe.

80. ***I*** , a pronoun.
***Aye or ay***, yes.

*Eye*, organ of sight.

81. ***Indite***, to compose and write.
***Indict***, to charge or accuse formally.

82. ***Isle***, a contraction for island.
***Aisle***, passage in an auditorium.
***I'll***, contraction for "I will, l".

83. ***Kernel***, the central part.
***Colonel***, chief officer of a regiment.

84. ***Lane***, a narrow passage.
***Lain***, past participle of lie, to rest lengthwise on or against.

85. ***Leaf***, as of a book, a tree, etc.
***Lief***, willingly.

86. ***Least***, little; beyond all others.
***Leased***, held on lease.

87. ***Led***, past tense and participle of lead.
***Lead***, a metal.

88. ***Liar***, one who tells lies.
***Lyre***, a musical instrument.

89. ***Lone***, solitary; alone.
***Loan***, a temporary grant.

90. ***Male***, opposite of female.
***Mail***, armour; letters.

91. ***Mane***, the long hair on the neck of an animal.
***Main***, the sea; principal; chief.

92. ***Manner***, method or way.
***Manor***, an estate; a domain.

93. ***Mantle***, a clock; a cover.
***Mantel***, the slab or shelf above a fireplace.

94. ***Marshal***, a military or police officer.
***Martial***, warlike.

95. ***Maze***, an intricate place.
***Maize***, Indian corn.

96. ***Mean***, shabby; low; to intend.
***Mien***, manner of look or appearance.

97. ***Meet***, fit; to assemble.
***Mete***, to measure.
***Meat***, food; flesh.

98. ***Mind***, thc understanding.
***Mined***, execavated.

99. ***Miner***, a worker in mine.
***Minor***, one under age.

100. ***Mite***, something very small.
***Might***, power; strength.

101. ***Moan***, to lament.
***Mown***, cut down.

102. ***Mussel***, a shellfish.
***Muscle***, the fleshy parts of an animal body.

103. ***Mustard***, a kind of plant.
***Mestered***, assembled.

104. ***Nave***, hub of a wheel; main portion of a cathedral.

*Knave*, a rogue.

105. ***May***, no.
***Meigh***, cry of a horse.

106. ***Need***, want; poverty.
***Knead***, to work the materials into dough.

107. ***New***, not old.
***Knew***, pat tense of know.
***Gnu***, a wild ox.

108. ***Night***, opposite of day.

109. ***Knight***, a title of honour.

110. ***No***, opposite of yes.
***Know***, to understand.

111. ***Nose***, the organ of smell.
***Noes***, plural of no.
***Knows***, has knowledge: understands.

112. ***Oar***, implement for rowing a boat.
***Ore***, metal as it comes from the earth.
***O'er***, contraction for over.

113. ***Ode***, a short poem.
***Owed***, indebted to: past tense of owe.

114. ***Our***, a pronoun.
***Hour***, sixty minutes.

115. ***Pain***, soreness.
***Pane***, a piece of glass.

116. ***Pair***, two a couple.
***Pare***, to slice thinly.
***Pear***, a kind of fruit.

117. ***Passed***, gone through; gone.
***Past***, not present or future.

118. ***Pause***, a stop.
***Paws***, feet of a beast.

119. ***Peace***, a state of quiet.
***Piece***, a part.

120. ***Pedal***, a foot lever to operate such a lever.
***Peddle***, to sell from house to house

121. ***Peel***, skin, outside.
***Peal***, sound of bells.

122. ***Peer***, to look intently: an equal.
***Pier***, a wharf.

123. ***Plane***, a perfectly flat or level surface; a kind of tree.
***Plain***, level flat country.

124. ***Plate***, a flat piece of metal; a shallow dish.
***Plait***, to fold to braid.

125. ***Please***, to delight or gratify.
***Pleas***, pleadings in law: excuses.

126. ***Plum***, a fruit.
***Plumb***, perpendicular: an instrument to determine whether a wall is perpendicular.

127. ***Pray***, to entreat.
***Prey***, plunder.

128. ***Prays***, supplicates.
***Praise***, approbation: to approve.
***Preys***, attacks, as a wild beast.

129. ***Principal***, invested funds; chief.

***Principle***, a fundamental rule or law.

130. ***Quarts***, measures of two pints each.
***Quartz***, a variety of rock crystal.

131. ***Rain***, water from clouds.
***Rein***, part of a harness; to check.
***Reign***, to rule as a king.

132. ***Rap***, to strike sharply.
***Wrap***, to wind or roll together: to fold.

133. ***Rapped***, struck.
***Rapt***, transported: ravished.
***Wrapped***, folded; enclosed.

134. ***Rays***, beams of light.
***Raise***, to exalt: to lift up.
***Raze***, to destroy utterly.

135. ***Read***, as a book: to study.
***Reed***, a hollow cane.

136. ***Red***, a colour.
***Read***, past tense of read.

137. ***Rest***, peace; quiet.
***Wrest***, to twist: to wrench.

138. ***Right***, just: correct.
***Rite***, a ceremony.
***Write***, to trace letters or characters.
***Wright***, a workman.

139. ***Road***, a path; a way.
***Rode***, past tense of ride.
***Rowed***, propelled with oars.

140. ***Role***, a part in acting a play.
***Roll***, a round thing; a register.

141. ***Rood***, fourth part of an acre.
***Rude***, uncultivated : rough.
***Rued***, grieved for.

142. ***Root***, as of a plant: origin.
***Route***, direction: road.

143. ***Ruff***, an article of dress.
***Rough***, unpolished: rugged.

144. ***Rung***, sounded as a bell.
***Wrung***, twisted.

145. ***Rye***, a sort of grain.
***Wry***, crooked.

146. ***Sac***, a membranous receptacle.
***Sack***, a large strong bag.

147. ***Sail***, to navigate.
***Sale***, act of selling.

148. ***Sea***, a wide expanse of water.
***See***, to perceive.

149. ***Seam***, a line of junction between pieces of cloth.
***Seem***, to appearance to have a semblance.

150. ***Sees***, looks at.
***Seize***, to take hold of.
***Skull***, the whole bone of the head.

151. ***Scull***, a small boat; a light, short oar.
152. ***Soared***, mounted on the wing.
***Sword***, a weapon of war.
153. ***Sold***, given for a price.
***Soled***, furnished with a sole.
154. ***Sore***, painful.
***Soar***, to mount by flight.
155. ***Soul***, the spirit.
***Sole***, only bottom of the foot: a fish.
156. ***Sow***, to scatter seed.
***Sew***, to fasten as with a needle.
***So***, in this manner.
157. ***Staid***, steady grave.
***Stayed***, supported with ropes as a mast.
158. ***Stair***, flight of steps.
***Stare***, to look at.
159. ***Stake***, a pointed piece of wood.
***Steak***, a slice of meat.
160. ***Straight***, direct: not curved.
***Strait***, narrow: confined.
161. ***Style***, manner of dress or action.
***Stile***, steps over a wall.
***Sucker***, a young shoot of a tree.
162. ***Succour***, help to relieve.
***Sum***, the amount of anything; to add up.
***Some***, more or less of a quantity.
163. ***Sutler***, one who follows a camp to sell provisions, etc.
***Subtler***, more cunning; more acute.
164. ***Sweet***, pleasant delightful.
***Suite***, attendants a set of rooms.
165. ***Tale***, a story.
***Tail***, an appendage: hinder part.
166. ***Taught***, past tense and perfect participle of teach.
***Taut***, streteched light.
167. ***Tear***, water from the eye.
***Tier***, a row: a series.
168. ***Teem***, to produce in abundance.
***Team***, a pair of horses or oxen, working together.
169. ***Their***, possessive of they.
***There***, adv., in that place.
170. ***Threw***, past tense of throw.
***Through***, from side to side or from end to end.
***Throw***, to east; to fling.
***Throe***, extreme pain.
171. ***Time***, fit season.
***Thyme***, a garden plant.
172. ***Told***, expressed in words.

*Tolled*, rung as a bell.

173. ***Tract***, a quantity of land.
***Tracked***, followed by the marks left.

174. ***Two***, a pair twice one.
***Too***, *adv.*, also: excess as too much.
***To***, preposition.

175. ***Use***, to apply or handle for some purpose.
***Owes***, female sheep.
***Yews***, evergreen trees.

176. ***Vale***, a valley.
***Vell***, a curtain a covering.

177. ***Vice***, a fault.
***Vise***, a tool.

178. ***Wade***, to walk through water.
***Weighed***, past tense of weight

179. ***Wait***, to remain: to stay.
***Weight***, heviness; importance.

180. ***Ware***, sing of wares; goods.
***Wear***, to last: to endure.

181. ***Waste***, to squander.
***Waist***, the middle part as of the body.

182. ***Wave***, a moving ridge: to undulate.
***Waive***, to defer: to abandon.

183. ***Way***, a road: manner.
***Weigh***, to determine heaviness: to ponder.

184. ***Wood***, a forest; timber.
***Would***, verb of wish or determination.

# HETERONYMS

Words spelled the same but differing in sound and in meaning. Strictly, *heteronyms*, from the very etymology of the word, have no alliance between them except the accidental one of the same orthography. They are derived from different roots and their meanings are so distinct that their separate origin is at once indicated by such meanings. Mere change of accent, moreover does not constitute a heteronym.

***Bass*** *(bās)*, a term in music.
***Bass*** *(bas)*, a fish.
***Bow*** *(bou)*, the forward part of a vessel.
***Bow*** *(bō)*, an archer's weapon; an implement for playing the violin; a knot.
***Chap*** *(chăp)*, a fellow.
***Chap*** *(chŏp)*, fleshy covering of a jaw.
***Dives*** *(divz)*, goes under water.
***Dives*** *(di´vēz)*, the rich man.
***Does*** *(dōz)*, female deer.
***Does*** *(dŭz)*, from the verb do.
***Gill*** *(jĭl)*, quarter of a pint.
***Gill*** *(gĭl)*, the organ of respiration of fish.
***Glower*** *(glu´ēr)*, to stare.
***Glower*** *(glō´ēr)*, something that glows.
***Hinder*** *(hĭn´dēr)*, to prevent.
***Hinder*** *(hin´dēr)*, back part.
***Job*** *(jŏb)*, petty work.
***Job*** *(jōb)*, a man´s name.
***Lead*** *(lid)*, a man´s name.

***Lead** (lēd)*, to conduct.
***Lower** (lō´ẽr)*, to descend.
***Lower** (lou´ẽr)*, to frown.
***Manes** (mãnz)*, the hair on the neck of animals.
***Manes** (mā´nēz)*, departed spirits.
***Mate** (māt)*, a companion.
***Mate** (mä´tā)*, a beverage.
***Mow** (mō)*, to cut down.
***Mow** (mou)*, heap of grain a compartment for storing grain.
***Mowing** (mŏ´ĭng)*, the act of cutting.
***Mowing** (mou´ĭng)*, to store away.
***Polish** (pŏl´ĭsh)*, to shine.
***Polish** (pŏl´ĭsh)*, adjective derived from Pole-pertaining to Poland.
***Poll** (pŏl)*, a degree without honors.
***Poll** (pōl)*, the head; a tax.
***Put** (pōōt)*, to move; to push.
***Put** (pŭt)*, a rustic: a clown.
***Repent** (rē´pĕnt)*, creeping: prostrate: reptant.
***Repent** (re-pĕnt´) to fe)*, el pentitence, contrition, or regret, for what one has done or has omitted to do.
***Row** (rō)*, a rank or file; to propel with oars.
***Row** (rou)*, a tumult.
***Sake** (sāk)*, purpose, end, cause.
***Sake** (sä´kē)*, liquor made from rice.
***Sewer** (sū´ẽr)*, a ditch or a drain.
***Sewer** (sö´èr), one who sews.*
***Shower** (shö´èr)*, one that exhibits.
***Shower** (shou´èr), light rain.*
***Singer** (sĭn´jèr)*, one that singes.
***Singer** (sĭng´er)*, one that sings.
***Slough** (slou, sloo)*, a hole full of mire; a marshy place.
***Slough** (slŭf)*, cast-off skin of a serpent.
***Sow** (sō)*, to scatter seeds.
***Sow** (sou)*, female pig.
***Stingy** (stĭn´jĭ)*, penurious.
***Stingy** (stĭng´ĭ)*, piercing.
***Swinger** (swĭng´ẽr)*, one that swings.
***Swinger** (swĭn´jẽr)*, one that beats or chastises.
***Tarry** (tär´ĭ)*, covered with or like, tar.
***Tarry** (tăr´ĭ)*, to abide at or in a place; to say; to loiter to delay.
***Tear** (târ)*, to divide or separate on being pulled.
***Tear** (tēr)*, a drop of limpid saline fluid secreted by the lachrymal gland.
***Tower** (tou´ẽr)*, a high edifice; a citadel.
***Tower** (tō´èr)*, that which tows.
***Wind** (wĭnd)*, air in motion.
***Wind** (wīnd)*, to twist.
***Wound** (wōōnd)*, an injury.
***Wound** (wound)*, twisted.